COLIN,

BEST WISHES FOR 2005

FROM. George & Sidonia.

THE NATIONAL PARKS
and Other Wild Places of
BRITAIN
and
IRELAND

The National Parks
and Other Wild Places of
BRITAIN
and
IRELAND

JONATHAN ELPHICK • DAVID TIPLING

NEW HOLLAND

First published in 2002 by New Holland Publishers (UK) Ltd
London • Cape Town • Sydney • Auckland

Garfield House, 86–88 Edgware Road, London W2 2EA, United Kingdom
www.newhollandpublishers.com
80 Mckenzie Street, Cape Town 8001, South Africa
Level 1/Unit 4, 14 Aquatic Drive, Frenchs Forest NSW 2086 Australia
218 Lake Road, Northcote, Auckland, New Zealand

10 9 8 7 6 5 4 3 2

ISBN 1 85974 898 8

Publishing Manager: Jo Hemmings
Project Editor: Camilla MacWhannell
Editorial Assistant: Daniela Filippin
Copy Editor: Sue Viccars
Design: Alan Marshall
Cartography: William Smuts
Production: Joan Woodroffe

Reproduction by Pica Digital Pte Ltd, Singapore
Printed and bound in Singapore by Star Standard Industries (Pte) Ltd

Publishers' Note
Throughout this book, species are, where possible, referred to by their common
rather than their scientific names for ease of reference by the general reader.
Where no common names exist, scientific names are used. Many of the titles
listed in the further reading section on page 173 provide full scientific names
for species found in Britain and Ireland. The maps contained in the book are
intended as 'locators' only; detailed, large-scale maps should be
consulted when planning a trip. It is important to note that access, accommodation, and other details vary as new transport methods and facilities develop.
Remember that trail routes can vary, river courses can change, and water
depths can alter dramatically within minutes. Although the publishers and
author made every effort to ensure that the information in this book was
correct at the time of going to press, they accept no responsibility for any loss,
injury or inconvenience sustained by any person using the book.

Illustrations appearing in the preliminary pages are as follows: half title: Grey
Seal; title pages: Loch Slapin & Cullin Hills Isle of Skye, Scotland; pages 4-5:
Ullswater, Lake District, Northern England; pages 6-7 (l to r): Mountain Hare,
Natterjack Toad, Otter, Mute Swan, Badger, Barn Owl; pages 8-9: Marwick
Head RSPB Reserve, Mainland Orkney, Scotland.

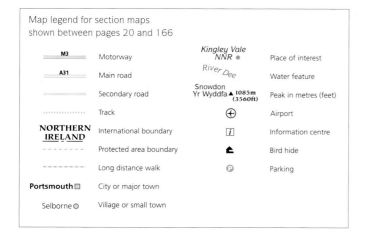

Map legend for section maps
shown between pages 20 and 166

M3	Motorway	Kingley Vale NNR ●	Place of interest
A31	Main road	River Dee	Water feature
	Secondary road	Snowdon Yr Wyddfa ▲ 1085m (3560ft)	Peak in metres (feet)
	Track	⊕	Airport
NORTHERN IRELAND	International boundary	[i]	Information centre
	Protected area boundary	☚	Bird hide
	Long distance walk	℗	Parking
Portsmouth ☐	City or major town		
Selborne ◎	Village or small town		

CONTENTS

FOREWORD

North, south, east and west, you hold the best of the wilder places of Great Britain and Ireland in your hands. From the Shetlands to the Scillies, the Norfolk Broads to Killarney's National Park these are living landscapes where history both natural and people made are still working together in some sort of harmony. Tempting as it is to use the word wilderness, it would be untrue, for the length and breadth of these islands have been witness to the tread of humankind for many millennia. Seven thou-

sand years ago the vast majority of these lands were covered by Native Forest. Great oaks and pines obscured all inland views and open grassland was confined to sand dunes. Other places where the wind blew and water flowed reigned supreme and were the most favoured spots for deer and aurochs to graze safely. It was the discovery of how to polish the stone of the Langdale Pikes in what we now call the Lake District National Park, that turned our Neolithic ancestors from hunter gatherers into farmers. From that point on, trees began to fall, new vistas were opened up and the landscapes

highlighted in this wonderful book became as much a part of history as wars and rumours of peace.

Thank God for John Muir's vision of National Parks, of the sanctity of landscapes that nurture pride of place, the very roots of nationhood in all its biodiversity. Thank God too for the hard work of all the people who have and still keep this vision alive.

Wow! These are not just snapshots; they are Windows of Wonder, allowing us to make links between the past, the present and the right decisions for all our futures. What better time to bring all this information together than now, as partnerships of people across the world are beginning to work to restore the balance of their own degraded lands.

I like to call this mass movement of people working with nature, the Green Renaissance. Turn these pages with the care they deserve for they contain vital information of a unique resource, the wisdom of the past linked to the last natural gene banks of the present, the key resource with which we can restore and build a more balanced future.

David Bellamy

DAVID BELLAMY, BEDBURN

INTRODUCTION

The British Isles lie on the western part of the continental shelf of Europe, separated from the main European landmass in the south by the English Channel – 35 kilometres (21 miles) wide at its narrowest point – and in the east by the North Sea.

Britain (or Great Britain) is the largest island, consisting of England, Wales and Scotland (all in the United Kingdom/UK). Across the Irish Sea to the west lies the island of Ireland, comprising Northern Ireland (part of the UK), and the independent Irish Republic, covering four-fifths of the island's area. There are also more than 1,000 offshore islands in the British Isles, mainly off the west and north of Scotland. This, and the irregular margins of the mainland, accounts for over 19,000 kilometres (12,000 miles) of coastline.

Unlike many of the countries covered in this series of books, but in common with other densely populated regions, the British Isles have few wilderness areas in the absolute sense of the word: that is, places that have been unchanged by man. However, these islands do have an abundance of places where one can escape modern life and enjoy magnificent scenery and exciting wildlife. For variety of landscapes in such a small area the British Isles has no equal.

Within a few days, the lover of wild places can explore lonely windswept beaches, rolling farmland with picturesque historic villages, tranquil lakes, stately rivers and rushing streams, flower-rich heaths, and woodlands ringing with birdsong. The choice is endless, from the wildlife-rich islands of the Pembrokeshire coast or the Outer Hebrides, the dramatic mountains and moorlands of Wales or the Scottish Highlands, and the great blanket bogs of the Flow Country of northeast Scotland and western Ireland, to the ancient woodland and heath of the New Forest.

Right: *Hay meadows in the Yorkshire Dales are home to a variety of flora such as buttercups, Bloody Cranes-bill and Wood Sorrel.*

The British Isles have some of the most beautiful sea coasts in Europe: great estuaries echoing to the haunting cries of waders and wildfowl, unspoilt sandy beaches with stretches of windswept dunes, huge expanses of shifting shingle, seabird-thronged cliffs and remote islands.

The British have for generations appreciated the beauty of the countryside and its wildlife, and the importance of conservation, resulting in a great range of National Parks and conservation areas.

Cultural Diversity

Repeated waves of invasion and immigration throughout history – from Celts, Romans, Angles, Saxons, Vikings, Normans and Jews to more recent arrivals from all over the world – have resulted in cultural diversity. While many of the immigrant communities retain their native languages, English is spoken almost universally, but with a range of accents. There are many local dialects, such as those of the south-western counties of Devon, Cornwall and Somerset, or the Northumberland dialect in north-east England, and the regional dialects of Scottish and Irish English. Thousands of people still speak Celtic languages. In Wales, Welsh is spoken by half a million people. Scottish Gaelic is used regularly by fewer than 1.5 per cent of the Scottish population, while in Ireland about 2 per cent speak Irish Gaelic.

As a result different names are given to landscape features around the islands: for example, a lake is a llyn in Wales, a loch in Scotland and a lough in Ireland. Signposts, street names, and other information are often printed first in Celtic, with the English translation beneath.

Below: *Rolling hills, untouched grasslands and downland flora on the South Downs.* Below, right: *The stark landscape of the lower slopes of the Glyders in Snowdonia National Park, Wales.*

Climate

Although lying on the same latitude as chilly Newfoundland or Moscow, the islands' climate is mild, thanks to the warming influence of the Gulf Stream, a current that sweeps northwards past the western shores. In the coastal areas of the southwest of England, Wales and Ireland, winters are generally frost-free and plants more typical of subtropical climes flourish. The west is wetter than the east, and the north cooler than the south, though the cooling effects of altitude also come into play. The exposed north and northwest of Scotland generally receives the most wind and rain.

The weather can be notoriously changeable from day to day or, in upland areas, even from hour to hour. It is advisable always to travel with a change of clothes, including warm and rainproof garments, and to check the short-range weather forecasts daily on radio, TV or in the newspapers.

Natural Riches

The ever-changing patchwork of different habitats provides opportunities for a great variety of wildlife and vegetation to flourish. Some 60 species of mammals occur, including marine mammals such as Bottlenose Dolphins and two species of seal. Most of the land mammals are difficult to see, being relatively small, hidden or well camouflaged, and often nocturnal. Notable exceptions are the deer, including the largest native mammal, the Red Deer, and the Rabbit.

The British Isles is renowned for its birdlife. Over 560 species have been recorded – almost three-quarters of the total for Europe – although over half of these are scarce or rare wanderers; about 260 species occur regularly, including about 135 species of year-round residents and about 125 species of summer and winter visitors and passage migrants annually.

Especially well represented are wintering wildfowl and waders on wetlands and estuaries, and seabirds breeding along the coasts, especially along the seacliffs of north and west Britain and the west of Ireland.

Although the British Isles has fewer species of birds of prey than much of Europe, those that do breed include the magnificent Golden Eagle (all but one pair in Scotland) and the Red Kite, native to mid Wales and reintroduced to various parts of England and Scotland.

The British Isles is also a superb place to watch bird migration in spring and autumn, when migrants arrive to breed or spend winter here, leave to winter further south, or stop off briefly on passage.

There are six native species each of reptiles and amphibians. The reptiles include three snakes, including the venomous Adder, the only potentially dangerous native wild land animal in the islands. There are no snakes in Ireland.

The freshwaters of Britain and Ireland contain over 50 species of fish. Another 190 or so marine species have been identified in inshore waters.

There are over 20,000 species of insects, including more than 4,000 species of beetles, over 60 of butterflies, over 2,300 of moths, and about 40 of dragonflies and damselflies. Other invertebrates are also well represented: there are over 600 species of spiders.

Although species have disappeared with modern farming methods, there are still over 1,500 species of wildflowers, a fascinating mixture of those typical of northwest and southern Europe, and Arctic-Alpine species. There are 35 native species of broadleaved trees, including some of the most splendid and ancient trees in Europe, three native conifers (the Scots Pine, Yew and Juniper), and many more introduced species. The mild, moist climate encourages a rich flora of ferns, horsetails, mosses and liverworts, and a great variety of fungi and lichens.

Conserving the Natural Heritage

The long history of conservation here includes a strong tradition of amateur involvement. The so-called 'mass trespass' of Kinder Scout in the Peak District in spring 1932 was made by ramblers protesting at the lack of public rights of way, and resulted in the imprisonment of five of the organizers.

The protest this aroused helped towards the creation of England's first National Park, the Peak District, in 1951, after parliament's National Parks and Access to the Countryside Act in 1949. This Act also established the National Parks Commission (now the Countryside Agency).

There are 11 National Parks in England and Wales, including The Broads in East Anglia (which gained equivalent National Park status in 1989). The New Forest and the South Downs have also been proposed for National Park status. These are all described in this book. There are no National Parks in Northern Ireland or Scotland. However, the recently devolved Scottish parliament plans to create its first Park in the beautiful Loch Lomond and the Trossachs area.

The Irish Republic has six National Parks; in addition to the three covered here, they include Glenveagh National Park (County Donegal), Connemara National Park (County Galway), and Mayo National Park, County Mayo.

A crucial difference between British National Parks and those in much of the rest of the world is that they are not 'national' in

Below, left: *Snow covers the ancient Caledonian Pine Forest at Loch an Eilean in Speyside, Scotland.* Below: *The spectacular Torc Waterfall in Killarney National Park, Ireland.*

the sense of public ownership: most of the land is in private hands, and access is sometimes restricted. Furthermore, they are not kept as wilderness areas devoid of people, but are home to working communities.

Areas of Outstanding Natural Beauty (AONBs) receive more limited protection and there is no statutory right of overall public access: there are over 50 in England, Wales and Northern Ireland. Scotland has 40 National Scenic Areas (NSAs) with similar status.

Other areas of conservation importance include the 35 per cent of coastline of England and Wales designated as Heritage Coasts; over 100 Ramsar sites (designated wetlands); UNESCO World Heritage sites (including The Giant's Causeway in Northern Ireland, the remote islands of St Kilda west of Scotland, and Hadrian's Wall in Northumberland, north-east England).

There are more than 6,000 government-designated Sites (or in Northern Ireland, Areas) of Special Scientific Interest (SSSIs/ASSIs). In the Republic of Ireland, the equivalent areas are called Natural Heritage Areas (NHAs), of which over 1,000 have been identified. Unfortunately, despite their legal status, many SSSIs, ASSIs and NHAs are frequently threatened by development.

Special Areas of Conservation (SACs) protect habitats and wildlife, while Special Protection Areas (SPAs) protect breeding or wintering birds. Together, the hundreds of SACs and SPAs form part of Europe's Natura 2000 network of conservation sites.

There are over 300 National Nature Reserves (NNRs) in the UK, all SSSIs/ASSIs and managed for public access by government conservation bodies (English Nature, Scottish Natural Heritage and the Countryside Council for Wales) or by independent bodies such as the National Trust and the National Trust for Scotland. The Republic of Ireland also has statutory nature reserves and six Refuges for Fauna.

Below: *The majestic Red Kite can now be seen in various parts of Britain.* Below, centre: *The Brown Long-eared Bat.* Below, right: *The Lumpsucker spends most of its time clinging to rocks.*

There are also many local nature reserves and country parks, under the control of district councils or other local bodies.

Many other reserves are owned or leased by conservation organizations, such as the Royal Society for the Protection of Birds (RSPB), whose 150 sites protect a wide range of habitats and special birds. The Wildfowl and Wetlands Trust (WWT) has nine regional centres, each with reserves for wintering wildfowl, featuring captive collections of wildfowl and research and education facilities.

A further 2,300 reserves are cared for by the 46 Wildlife Trusts, while the National Trust owns over 248,000 hectares (612,000 acres) of countryside and nearly 1,000 kilometres (600 miles) of coastline in England, Wales and Northern Ireland; the National Trust for Scotland owns 73,000 hectares (180,000 miles) of countryside in Scotland.

Visiting Protected Areas in the British Isles

This book covers a selection of National Parks and other protected areas open to the public. When planning a visit, contact the relevant authority (see page 172) for further details.

Accommodation is available locally for all the sites, though it is wise to book ahead, especially in summer. There is usually a wide range of places to stay, from campsites and Youth Hostels to 'bed-and-breakfast' establishments, welcoming inns, known as 'pubs' (public houses), self-catering cottages and luxurious hotels.

Another option is to book a holiday geared to enjoying wild places, wildlife and plants, or on a course at a Field Studies Council centre in England and Wales, or to take part in practical conservation at a reserve or as part of the BTCV working holidays.

Wildlife Watching and Botanizing

The British Isles was the birthplace of the modern study of natural history, producing a great number of gifted naturalists, from Gilbert White, the great 18th-century parson-naturalist, to more recent pioneers such as Julian Huxley, James Fisher, David Bellamy and Sir David Attenborough.

There is a thriving interest in natural history, with a huge number of local societies, clubs and voluntary organizations, as well as national ones, devoted to all aspects of the field. The RSPB, for example, has over a million members.

Visitor Activities

Visitors can enjoy a great range of activities, from guided tours of nature reserves, castles or prehistoric sites to hang-gliding and pony trekking. There is an excellent system of long-distance footpaths for walkers, as well as countless paths, green lanes and abandoned railway tracks. Cycling is another good way of seeing the countryside, aided by an increasing network of routes. Horse riding has a long tradition, and there are thousands of kilometres of bridleways.

Rock climbing is popular; there is a huge range of climbs, from the easiest scrambles to the most challenging ascents. There are thousands of caves and potholes for experienced cavers to explore in limestone regions such as those in south Wales, the Pennines, and the west of Ireland.

Devotees of watersports are well catered for with sailing on many coasts, lakes and reservoirs, and canoeing on rivers. A great way to see wildlife along canals and rivers is to hire a houseboat. Scuba diving is increasingly popular, revealing superb underwater landscapes with rich marine communities as well as some of the world's most important wreck sites. Surfing, though relatively limited, is possible, especially along the coasts of Devon, Cornwall, the Gower and northeast England.

Local Life

This is very much a working countryside, moulded by the many people who live there. The intimate and often ancient relationships that have developed between country people and the landscape and its fauna and flora are expressed in many ways, with distinct regional differences, such as the drystone walls typical of the Lake District or Yorkshire Dales, or the rolling grouse moors of northern England and Scotland

Threats to Natural Habitats and Wildlife

Over the millennia, the original wild woodland that covered much of the British Isles was steadily felled and the land largely tamed by drainage and cultivation or grazing animals. The great majority of landscapes are managed, mostly as farmland, and increasing areas are taken up by housing, road systems and other developments.

In particular, the development of modern intensive agriculture during the 20th century, especially since the 1950s, has resulted in profound alterations in the rural environment and wildlife. This includes the removal of thousands of kilometres of ancient, ecologically rich hedgerows to create larger fields for the increasingly large-scale machinery used to produce arable crops.

Grassland 'improvement' has had drastic effects on wildflowers and animals, and much damage has resulted from drainage of ponds and wetlands, woodland clearance and reclamation of heathland and moorland. Birds are very good indicators of the general health of the land, and many common species have suffered declines of up to 80 per cent or more.

With over 80 per cent of visits to the countryside made by car, there is an urgent need to encourage greater use of public transport, but many rural areas suffer from inadequate bus services and unreliable railway links.

Many of the most popular beauty spots are literally being worn away by the pressure of traffic, both from cars and the tramp of millions of feet, resulting in erosion, disturbance of breeding species and damage to the environment and its wildlife.

But wildlife can be remarkably resilient, and there is a huge and growing interest in conservation. Hopefully this will win out, and the priceless natural treasures of the British Isles will survive for generations of visitors to enjoy in the future.

Below left: *Fruits of the Sweet Chestnut in autumn.* Below, centre: *The aptly-named Bee Orchid.* Below, right: *Yellow pansies flowering on the dunes at Newborough Warren in Wales.*

The National Parks and Other Wild Places of Britain and Ireland

KEY

▭	Motorway
	Main road
— · — · —	International boundary
━━━━	National boundary
————	County boundary
COVENTRY ▫	City or major town
Gloucester ○	Town
	Water feature

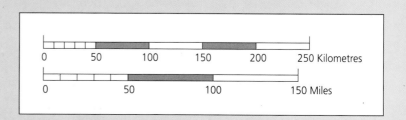

Westport○

Aran Islands

Cliffs of Moher

Bridges of Ross

Ra○
Abbeyfeale○
Tralee○ ○ Ca
Killarney○
KERRY ㉜
Skelligs   Macro

Cape Clear

ATLANTIC OCEAN

0	50	100	150	200	250 Kilometres

0	50	100	150 Miles

SOUTH-WEST ENGLAND

THIS DISTINCTIVE PART OF ENGLAND encompasses the area traditionally known as the West Country, usually covering the counties of Cornwall, Devon and Somerset. As defined here, this also includes Dorset and Wiltshire to the east.

Much of this 19,542-square-kilometre (7,546-square-mile) area falls within a long, gradually narrowing peninsula protruding into the Atlantic Ocean, culminating in the rocky promontory of Land's End and the beautiful heath-rich plateau of The Lizard.

It contains some of the most spectacular coastal scenery in the British Isles, much of it

designated as AONBs, owned by the National Trust or protected in some way. There are also romantic islands to explore: the peaceful, sunny Isles of Scilly, west of Land's End, and dramatic Lundy, with towering sea cliffs, in the Bristol Channel.

Inland, too, the region has much to offer, from Dartmoor in Devon and Bodmin Moor in Cornwall – wild, windswept moorlands with weathered granite outcrops called tors – to varied landscapes of pastoral farming, tumbling rivers and sheltered wooded valleys, ringing with birdsong.

There are two National Parks in the region: Dartmoor in Devon, the largest area of really wild country in southern England, and smaller, gentler Exmoor to the north, straddling Devon and Somerset.

The region enjoys the mildest climate in England, and is one of the country's most popular tourist destinations; the almost subtropical south coasts of south Devon and Cornwall are promoted as 'rivieras'. Yet it is always possible to escape the crowds and explore wilder places – such as the dramatic north coast, where the great Atlantic breakers pound the cliffs, or the more remote areas of Dartmoor, with sudden mists and desolate bogs.

Opposite top: *The delicate Silver-studded Blue Butterfly is mostly found on lowland heathland where it drinks nectar from flowers of Bell Heather, Crossleaved Heath and Bird's-foot Trefoil. It flies from late June to early August.*

Below: *South-west England is justly famed for its beautiful beaches, such as this unspoilt sandy bay on Tresco, Isles of Scilly.*

ISLES OF SCILLY

Birdwatcher's Paradise

Location: About 45 km (28 miles) west of Land's End, Cornwall.

Climate: Mild, frost-free in winter; warm, sunny in summer, but often windy and rainy.

When to Go: October best for rare migrant birds; to avoid birdwatching in a crowd, late March–May or August–September will guarantee commoner migrants, with a good chance of rarities. Spring sees maximum wildflower interest; summer is best for breeding seabirds.

Access: Daily boat from Penzance to St Mary's (2¾-hour journey); by air from Land's End (15 mins), summer only from Newquay (30 mins) and Plymouth (45 mins), and from Exeter (50 mins) and Bristol (1 hour 10 mins). Helicopter flights (about 20 mins) to St Mary's and Tresco from heliport 1.6 km (1 mile) east of Penzance. Local boats daily (weather permitting) between main islands.

Permits: Most uninhabited islands closed during bird breeding season (15 April–15 August). Landing prohibited all year on major seabird reserve of Annet; regular boat trips around it in summer. Stay away from breeding seals September–October.

Equipment: Waterproofs, fleece; diving and snorkelling gear.

Facilities: Variety of accommodation on inhabited islands; camping restricted. Book in advance.

Watching Wildlife: Outstanding birdwatching; excellent for botanists and entomologists; superb sea life for divers and snorkellers; Grey Seals, Porpoises, Dolphins and Basking Sharks often seen at sea.

Visitor Activities: Beaches, rock pools, swimming, sunbathing; walking, cycling, sailing, fishing.

The Isles of Scilly are a magical cluster of almost 200 little granite islands and rocks scattered across 18 kilometres (11 miles) of the Atlantic Ocean, a continuation of the exposed tops of a vast rock mass underlying much of the West Country. Some regard the islands as the remains of the legendary drowned Cornish kingdom of Lyonesse, but they have actually been settled since Bronze Age times, about 4,000 years ago, and are richly endowed with archaeological sites.

The smallest of England's AONBs, Scilly includes about 40 islands large enough to hold vegetation, including five inhabited ones: St Mary's, Tresco, St Agnes, Bryher and St Martin's. There are superb little coves, unspoiled beaches of dazzling white quartz sand, dunes and granite cliffs with dramatic views, and, inland, a patchwork of little fields, woodland and heather moorland, with an extensive network of peaceful, winding lanes and footpaths. The flatness of this miniature landscape – the highest point is just over 45 metres (150 feet), on St Mary's – combines with the great expanse of the ocean to give a wonderful feeling of space. Thanks to the lack of air pollution, the quality of the light is remarkably clear.

Top left: *Rare transatlantic autumn wanderers to Scilly have included Yellow-billed Cuckoos.*

Opposite, top: *This view across the island of St Martin's shows the range of habitats on the islands.*

Opposite, bottom: *A party of 'twitchers', keen to add a new bird to their lists, walk down a lane on the attractive island of St Mary's.*

The islands' shores have Heritage Coast status, and the area is a likely future marine nature reserve. The climate is very mild, thanks to their southerly position and the ameliorating influence of the Gulf Stream.

Island Variety

The biggest and most varied of the inhabited islands, St Mary's, home to over 80 percent of Scilly's 2,000 inhabitants, is only 4 kilometres (2½ miles) wide and 16 kilometres (10 miles) around the coast.

Much of Tresco, the second largest, was transformed by the Dorrien-Smith family, who introduced Elm, Sycamore and Monterey Pine to create shelter belts for flowers, including the exotic plants that grow in Abbey Gardens. This remarkable place, laid out in 1834, displays plants grown from seeds supplied by London's Kew Gardens, and from all over the world.

St Martin's has some of the best beaches, while Bryher's west coast is exposed to the full force of the Atlantic: in winter, the latter's Hell Bay lives up to its name. St Agnes is the most westerly of the inhabited islands, and includes three major birdwatching sites: Wingletang Down, the Old Parsonage Garden, and Periglis Beach.

Safe Haven

The islands are protected from the ravages of winter storms by a barrier of rocky reefs in the south west, towards their western limit at Bishop's Rock. These deflect the great Atlantic breakers, sending them upwards in an explosion of spray up to 30 metres (100 feet) high. This natural breakwater creates a haven of calm, warm, shallow water between the islands where beds of Eelgrass flourish. The sheltered shores of the northern islands provide a home for marine creatures usually found in deeper water,

Above: *Exotic plants flourish on the islands: this clump of Giant Tussock Sedge is on Higher Moors, St Mary's.*

Top right: *The Yellow-browed Warbler is the commonest Siberian vagrant to the Scilly Isles: most arrive in early October.*

Below: *Scilly migrants include insects as well as birds, such as this handsome Monarch butterfly from America.*

including Venus Clams and Purple Heart Urchins.

The storms proved a notorious hazard for ships, and more than 450 wrecks have been found, most dating back to the 1700s. These slowly decaying hulks provide excellent habitats for a rich variety of marine life, such as Devonshire Cup-corals and Jewel Anemones, which flourish in unpolluted waters so clear that the seabed can be visible by moonlight.

Islands of Flowers

Apart from tourism, the Scillonians make their living chiefly from fishing and the commercial growing of early flowers and vegetables for mainland markets. Thanks to the mild climate and long hours of sunshine – Scilly means 'sun islands'– golden Narcissi and purple Anemones can be grown as early as December, in little box-like fields protected by hedge-topped banks (known locally as 'fences') of Escallonia, Pittosporum and Veronica. However, the market gardening business has declined considerably in recent years.

Wildflowers are abundant, from the gaudy carpets of Mesembryanthemums, or Hottentot Figs, natives of South Africa, or the naturalized Narcissus, Agapanthus and Belladonna originating as discarded plants from the bulb fields, to native rarities such as Small Tree-mallow and Cornish Fumitory. Species like Common Poppies and Corn Marigolds, now rare arable weeds on much of the mainland, thrive here.

A Wealth of Wildlife

Hundreds of keen 'twitchers' gather on the islands during the peak migration season in autumn, often as an annual pilgrimage. Autumn rarities include migrants from Europe and Asia, or from North America, such as Buff-breasted Sandpipers and Yellow-billed Cuckoos, blown off course. Spring migration is on a smaller scale, but annually includes a few exotic-looking Golden Orioles and Hoopoes.

Scilly is also noted for breeding seabirds, especially on Annet Island: Manx Shearwaters, Shags, Storm-petrels, Fulmars, Kittiwakes, Guillemots, Puffins and Razorbills. There is a chance of seeing other species, such as Balearic, Sooty, Great or Cory's Shearwaters, Gannets and skuas, in early autumn, during the boat trip to and from the mainland.

Breeding landbirds include Wrens, Robins, Stonechats, Blackbirds and Sedge Warblers. Song Thrushes, suffering a dramatic decline on the mainland, are still abundant here, and are noticeably tame.

Grey Seals are a regular sight in summer, breeding in colonies mainly on the western rocks and especially on Annet. Porpoises and dolphins and huge, harmless Basking Sharks can be seen offshore. Land mammals include Rabbits, Wood Mice and Lesser White-toothed Shrews – the latter found elsewhere in the British Isles only in the Channel Islands.

Scilly is a great place to see migrant butterflies and moths in spring; as well as Clouded Yellow Butterflies and Hummingbird Hawk Moths, these occasionally include Monarch Butterflies from North America, blown off course from their normal migration to Mexico.

Threat from the Sea

Although the islands remain unpolluted and unspoilt, there is need for vigilance.

In 1967 the oil tanker *Torrey Canyon* ran aground off Scilly, resulting in the spillage of 100,000 tonnes of crude oil into the sea. This devastated many miles of the coasts of Cornwall, the Channel Islands and Brittany, France and caused serious damage to marine life. The powerful detergents used to disperse the oil proved more toxic to wildlife than the oil itself. An even greater threat comes from the cumulative discharge of small amounts of oil as a result of ships cleaning out their tanks.

LUNDY

Britain's First Marine Nature Reserve

This little, windswept, granite island lies at the mouth of the Bristol Channel where it meets the Atlantic Ocean. Only 5 kilometres (3 miles) long by 0.8 kilometre (½ mile) wide, with an area of just over 405 hectares (1,000 acres), it has fewer than 20 permanent residents, employed by the Landmark Trust, which manages the island for the National Trust. There are three lighthouses (two in use), one pub (the hub of island life), a well-stocked shop and no cars.

Lundy Island is flanked by towering cliffs up to 122 metres (390 feet) high along the north, west and south coasts. The east coast, facing the mainland, has steep slopes with small valleys, covered by bracken and intro-duced Rhododendron. The only relatively sheltered landing place lies in the south-east corner.

The flat central plateau is covered by grass and heather, with farmed land in the south and wild moorland to the north. It is grazed by rabbits, sheep (domestic sheep and Soay Sheep, an ancient breed introduced to the island in 1944), feral goats, Lundy Ponies and Sika Deer, originally from Japan and introduced in the 1920s. The deer live mainly among Rhododendron thickets on the east side, but can often be seen at dusk as they move towards the fields to feed. Black Rats, almost vanished from the British mainland, live on the appropriately named Rat Island off the south-east tip of Lundy.

Much scientific research into Lundy's wildlife and its conservation is organized by the Lundy Field Society; students and staff from Exeter University's School of Psychology visit the island to study animal behaviour.

Top right: *The beautiful Devonshire Cup Coral can be found in the sea off Lundy.*

Map labels

Kittiwake Gulley
Long Roost
North End
Gannets Bay
Threequarter Wall
Middle Park   Tibbetts Point
Lundy Island
Halfway Wall
Jenny's Cove
Punchbowl Valley   Quarries
Dead Cow Point
Quarter Wall
Battery Point
Ackland's Moor
Old Lighthouse   Village
Millcombe House
Landing Bay
Rat Island
South Lighthouse
Shutter Point

History

Lundy has a long and chequered past. Archaeologists have unearthed evidence of ancient settlements dating back to Neolithic or early Bronze Age times. Early Christians arrived during the Dark Ages, and Vikings raided the island. Next came the Normans, including the piratical de Marisco family, who built Marisco Castle and challenged the English King Henry III until Sir William de Marisco was captured and executed in 1242. The King reinforced Marisco Castle in an attempt to protect the island; the work was paid for by the sale of rabbits, for Lundy was one of the royal warrens. Despite this, the island continued as a hideaway for pirates, smugglers, convicts and plunderers of the many ships wrecked in the area. During the English Civil War (1642–9) it was a Royalist refuge, the last part of Britain to surrender to Cromwell's Roundheads.

Since then, Lundy has had a succession of owners. From 1836–1917 it was owned by the Heaven family, and became jokingly known as the 'Kingdom of Heaven'. More recently, Martin Coles Harman called himself 'King of Lundy', proclaimed the island a self-governing Dominion of the British Empire, and issued Lundy currency ('puffins') and postage stamps: stamps are still issued today, and are collectors' items. In 1969, the National Trust bought the island.

A Special Cabbage

Lundy is home to a variety of plants, including glorious pink Thrift, which carpets the clifftops in early spring. But the most special is the Lundy Cabbage, which – along with two species of beetles that live only on it – is found nowhere else in the world. The best place to look for this unique plant is around Millcombe House.

Location: 17.5 km (11 miles) off Hartland Point, north Devon.

Climate: Mild climate; frequent gales, rough seas and rain.

When to Go: Throughout year, for day trips or longer. Spring and autumn for migrant birds, summer for seabirds.

Access: The 300-ton MS *Oldenburg* (267 passengers) sails regularly all year from Bideford and in summer from Ilfracombe, (2 hours). Arrival/departure can be delayed by bad weather. Timetable of sailings/reserva-tions via Landmark Trust, Shottesbrooke, Maidenhead, Berkshire SL6 3SW. Tel: 01628 825925; Fax: 01628 825417. Very expensive helicopter flights (10 mins) from Lake Heliport, near Abbotsham, between Westward Ho! and Bideford.

Permits: None needed, but landing fee payable: included in the fare for MS *Oldenburg*.

Equipment: Walking/climbing equipment, waterproofs, fleece; diving and snorkelling gear.

Facilities: Self-catering in a variety of atmospheric renovated buildings, B&B via the Marisco Tavern or camping. No special facilities for disabled visitors: telephone in advance to arrange transportation up the hill to the 'village'. Information on accom-modation and other matters, including a guide book to the island, from the Landmark Trust (for details see Access, above).

Watching Wildlife: Birdwatching, mammal-watching, botanizing, searching for marine life in rock pools and underwater.

Visitor Activities: Walking, rock climbing (restricted during seabird breeding season), history/archaeology. Children usually fall in love with this island.

Opposite, right: *As well as providing a home for breeding seabirds and many plants, Lundy's dramatic cliffs, such as Seal Slab (foreground), provide tough challenges for rock climbers.*

The First Marine Reserve

Lundy is one of only two Marine Nature Reserves in Britain, and its clear waters and more than 200 wrecks are a magnet for divers and snorkellers. Administered by English Nature, the reserve extends from high-water mark to 1 kilometre (0.6 mile) offshore and features an underwater nature trail for scuba divers. Thanks to the great variety of underwater habitats ranging from sheer cliffs to large areas of sand and gravel, it is particularly rich in marine life, with many rare invertebrates. This undersea world resembles an aquatic garden, with brightly coloured seaweeds, sponges, cup corals, sea fans, jewel anemones and sea slugs, including many species more characteristic of the Mediterranean. Lundy is one of the few sites where all five native British species of corals can be found. Fish include Pollack, various wrasses and Red Bandfish, which spends much of its time buried in mud.

There is a small resident population of Grey Seals. They can be seen in the water or hauled out on the rocks, and breed in coves, such as Seal Hole on the south coast and at the foot of Puffin Gulley in the north. It is important to avoid disturbing them during their breeding season (September to November). Dolphins and Basking Sharks are regularly seen offshore in summer.

Rich Birdlife

Over 400 species of birds have been recorded. About 40 of these breed inland, including Peregrine Falcons, a few pairs of Lapwings and Curlews, Skylarks, Meadow and Rock Pipits, and Ravens. The main seabird colonies are along the west coast, especially at Battery Point, and on the northern tip. You can usually see Shags, Fulmars, Herring, Lesser Black-backed and Great Black-backed Gulls, Kittiwakes, and several hundred auks, mainly Guillemots and Razorbills.

The island was named by Norse raiders: Lunde-eye means 'Puffin Island'. These engaging birds have sadly now declined to just a few pairs, though non-breeders can be seen offshore. Large flocks (or 'rafts') of Manx Shearwaters gather offshore in summer, at night: most come from the breeding colonies on the Pembrokeshire islands, but some still breed on Lundy.

Most birdwatchers visit Lundy in spring and autumn to see migrants such as Merlins, Ring Ouzels, Short-eared Owls, Black Redstarts and other chats, a variety of warblers, and an impressive list of rarities. One or two Hoopoes and Golden Orioles are likely most years, particularly after light winds; Dotterels are recorded annually. Good sites for passerine migrants are the shrubs and overgrown quarries of the east side, and especially sheltered Millcombe Valley.

Lundy has claimed several 'firsts' for the British Isles. Most remarkable was the Ancient Murrelet that was first sighted in Jenny's Cove on 27 May 1990 by an astonished pair of birders on an RSPB trip, and which normally lives along the North Pacific coast. It probably crossed North America and then, finding itself in the wrong ocean, followed nesting auks to Lundy. It stayed until 26 June and, amazingly, returned the next two years.

Below: *The world's second largest fish, the Basking Shark, is a gentle giant that feeds solely on plankton.*

DARTMOOR NATIONAL PARK

Granite Heart of the West Country

Dartmoor is the largest and wildest open space in southern England. Most of it is a National Park (one of the earliest, established 1951) covering 954 square kilometres (368 square miles), almost half open moorland. Some 65 per cent overlies a great dome-shaped granite mass, thrust up about 295 million years ago, the easternmost emergence of subterranean granite that extends from beyond the Isles of Scilly. The softer sedimentary rocks that originally clothed this core have gradually been eroded over much of Dartmoor, and on the higher ground the granite, exposed to the elements, has formed rugged blocks – called tors. Over time the tough granite is shattered by frost into great piles of boulders known as clitters.

Together with the surrounding sedimentary sandstone, shale and limestone, this complex geology produces diverse habitats, supporting a wide variety of wildlife. The Park's boundaries also include the beautiful 'in-country' that fringes the

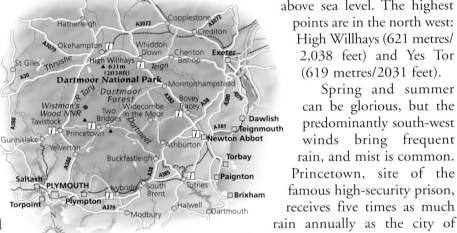

Top left: *Dartmoor is a stronghold of the Badger.*

Opposite, top left: *Clustered Bellflower.*

Opposite, centre left: *Hibernating Common Dormouse: these little mammals thrive in Dartmoor.*

Opposite, bottom left: *In early spring, Lesser Celandine carpets the ground in damp shady areas.*

Opposite, right: *The remains of the ancient clapper bridge at Dartmeet, along the East Dart river.*

moor proper: a patchwork of wooded river valleys, farms, small towns and villages, and moorland edge.

Climate and Human Influence

Over 50 per cent of the Park lies over 300 metres (984 feet) above sea level. The highest points are in the north west: High Willhays (621 metres/ 2,038 feet) and Yes Tor (619 metres/2031 feet).

Spring and summer can be glorious, but the predominantly south-west winds bring frequent rain, and mist is common. Princetown, site of the famous high-security prison, receives five times as much rain annually as the city of Exeter in east Devon. The exposed moor can be bitingly cold in winter; the trees that survive are twisted into strange shapes by the wind.

Despite its wildness, Dartmoor has long been affected by human activity that has moulded today's landscape: the moor holds the densest concentration of Bronze Age remains in North-west Europe, including the famous settlement at Grimspound, near Postbridge. Man's impact on the landscape has been through hunting, mining for tin and other metals, quarrying for granite, agricultural cultivation and stock-keeping, and the building of reservoirs.

The Open Moorland

The steeper well-drained slopes support Heather moorland and Bilberry. Crossleaved Heath and Purple Moor-grass are found in wetter spots, and yellow gorse in the driest areas. The familiar Common Gorse can be seen, but Western Gorse, which flowers later, is more prolific. In August the moor is a glorious sea of purple dotted with splashes of yellow.

Right: *The Stone Loach is a small, bottom-dwelling fish of unpolluted stony streams and rivers.*

Opposite, bottom right: *The layered nature of the granite helped form the characteristic Dartmoor tors, such as these outcrops of Combestone Tor on the eastern edge of the moor.*

Birds are generally sparsely distributed, with few remaining beyond autumn, but Buzzards and Ravens can often be seen overhead. Skylarks and Meadow Pipits are common, the latter the favourite host of the summer-visiting Cuckoos, laying eggs in their nests. Wheatears perch upright on the rocks, and the Ring Ouzel, at the southern limit of its British range, breeds in rocky areas on the higher moorland, but is declining. Dartmoor has never been managed as grouse moor, but there is a small, introduced population of Red Grouse on the wilder parts.

Foxes are relatively common, and best seen during early morning or at dusk. Adders, Britain's only venomous snakes, bask on boulders or stone walls on warm, sunny days.

Only the hardiest livestock can survive the bleak winters on the open moor. As well as tough breeds of sheep and cattle, the unique Dartmoor Ponies are an integral part of the moorland scene, and one is used as the Park's symbol. Few pure-bred animals remain; although wild they are all owned, and rounded up for stocktaking in annual autumn 'drifts'.

Deep Bogs
High rainfall, poor drainage and plant matter combine on the higher tops to produce deep blanket bogs, dominated by sphagnum mosses, Purple Moor Grass and cotton grasses. Small numbers of Golden Plover and Dunlin nest here at their southernmost breeding sites in Britain.

Bogs also develop in many valleys. These are richer communities than the blanket bogs: their many specialized plants include the insect-eating sundews and bladderworts, while animal life includes many dragonflies, Lapwings and Snipe.

Valley Woodlands and Upland Oakwoods
Consisting mainly of Oak, the valley woodlands support a rich wildlife. In spring they are carpeted with Bluebells, Daffodils and Wild Garlic, and echo to the sound of birdsong. Some birds, such as Tree Pipits, Wood Warblers, Redstarts and Pied Flycatchers, are migrant visitors: Woodcock, uncommon in south-west England, nest in places.

Pages 30–31: *Ancient oak woodland, Wistman's Wood National Nature Reserve, Dartmoor.*

Resident birds include all three species of British woodpeckers (Green, Great Spotted and the scarcer Lesser Spotted), Nuthatches, Treecreepers and tits.

A good range of woodland mammals include Red and Roe Deer and Common Dormice, while the limestone caves near Buckfastleigh contain major roosting and breeding sites for horseshoe bats. Badgers are common, especially at dusk.

Once, much of the moor was clothed with woodland. This was gradually cleared, and only a few beech copses and three relict areas of ancient oakwood – Black Tor Copse, Piles Copse and, most famous, Wistman's Wood – remain. This enchanting place, on a wild boulder-strewn slope, is a tangled mass of dwarf Pedunculate Oaks, with gnarled, twisted trunks and branches, festooned with lichens and mosses which thrive in the unpolluted air. Delicate white-flowered Wood Sorrel and woodrushes grow below the stunted oaks, some of which are descendants of trees dating back to the Stone Age.

Traditional Pastures and Hay Meadows
These are among Britain's most threatened habitats. The wet pastures are found alongside rivers in valley

bottoms and on shallow, poorly drained slopes, holding plants like Ivy-leaved Bellflower and Heath Spotted Orchid, and many scarce insects, such as Narrow-bordered Bee Hawkmoths and Marsh Fritillary butterflies.

Unaffected by modern agricultural practices, the ancient hay meadows support a host of lovely wildflowers, such as Yellow Rattle, Ox-eye Daisy and various orchids.

Reservoirs, Plantations and Rushing Waters

Dartmoor's eight artificial reservoirs (the only large stretches of standing water), filled with peaty, acidic water, are relatively poor in aquatic life, though their introduced fish attract wildfowl, notably Goosanders and Cormorants, and the occasional migrating Osprey in spring or autumn. A greater variety of birds including Goldcrests, Coal Tits and Siskins can be seen in the moor's conifer plantations.

Dartmoor is dissected with many fast-flowing streams and rivers, and most of Devon's rivers arise in a small area in the northern half of the moor. Streams and rivers are the haunts of Grey Herons,

Kingfishers, Dippers and Grey Wagtails. Otters are quite common but very elusive. American Mink, escapees from fur farms, are more often seen, and prey on waterfowl, their eggs and young.

During autumn floods Atlantic Salmon swim upriver from the sea to breed. Other fish include Brown Trout, Stone Loach and Miller's Thumb.

Above: *The Red Fox, known in the British Isles simply as the Fox, is often seen on Dartmoor.*

EXMOOR NATIONAL PARK

A Perfect Patchwork

Exmoor is one of Britain's smallest National Parks, covering 693 square kilometres (267 square miles). Designated in 1954, it is a mosaic of moorland, steep, narrow wooded valleys (combes) with fast-running, peat-stained rivers, a patchwork of farmland interspersed with small towns and villages, and rounded coastal hills plunging down to a wild coastline.

This varied landscape supports rich communities of wildlife, including over 1,000 species of wildflowers and grasses, more than 1,700 of insects (with over 1,000 moth species), and 31 species of native mammals. Over 240 bird species have been recorded, of which more than 100 breed and a further 50 are regular visitors.

In contrast to the granite of Dartmoor and Bodmin, Exmoor overlies sedimentary rocks, mainly sandstones, slates, grits and limestone. This gives the landscape a smoother, less forbidding aspect, though when blanketed by mist or rain or lying deep under snow, Exmoor can feel very remote.

Central Exmoor consists of a high plateau of heather and grass moorland. Its heartland, surrounding the little village of Simonsbath (pronounced 'Simmonsbath'), is known as Exmoor

Top left: *Scottish Blackface sheep, bred to cope with the harsh Scottish Highland weather, have been introduced to Exmoor.*

Opposite, top: *Badgworthy Water, the Doone Valley.*

Opposite, bottom left: *Primroses add a splash of colour to an Exmoor bankside.*

Opposite, bottom right: *A handsome male Redstart.*

Forest. This use of the word 'forest' is an ancient one, and in medieval times referred to land reserved for hunting by royalty. There have been few trees on Exmoor Forest since prehistoric settlers cleared the woods.

Heather moorland is found on the drier parts, especially the highest point at Dunkery Beacon (519 metres/1,703 feet). This is an important area for the localized Heath Fritillary butterfly. Resident Stonechats are common among the gorse and heather, while Whinchats returning to breed from Africa prefer the bracken-clad fringes. Among other summer visitors are small numbers of Ring Ouzels, Tree Pipits and Nightjars. More widespread are Skylarks, Meadow Pipits and Yellowhammers. The moor is also home to bigger birds, typically mewing Buzzards, hovering Kestrels and croaking Ravens. In winter these may be augmented by a hunting Short-eared Owl, Merlin or Hen Harrier.

Elsewhere burning and re-seeding produces grazing for sheep. The high north-western part of the moor is dominated by Purple Moor Grass, and can be very boggy, with Bog Pimpernel, Heath Spotted Orchid and Marsh Violet, the latter the food plant of Small Pearl-bordered Fritillary caterpillars.

Tough little Exmoor Ponies are the most obvious mammals on the moor, wintering in the sheltered combes. These are believed to be the British Isles' oldest native breed, nearest to the long-extinct original European wild horse, or Tarpan. Although they roam freely, these all have owners; two herds are owned by the National Park Authority. Look out for the harmless Hornet Robber-fly, Britain's

largest fly, on cattle-grazing areas; their dung provides its breeding grounds. Adders are often seen basking in the sun in sheltered spots.

Red Deer

Exmoor is the only area in England where Red Deer, the British Isles' largest wild land animal, have lived wild since prehistoric times (elsewhere they were hunted to extinction; they have been reintroduced in a few places), and today there are a few thousand. A stag's head was chosen as the Park's symbol. These magnificent animals are at the heart of a heated controversy between animal rights' activists and those who defend the Exmoor stag hunt as a traditional way of life and therefore vital to the area.

Wooded River Valleys

The moor is named after the River Exe, the West Country's longest river. It rises at a height of 442 metres (1,450 feet) at Exe Head among the boggy wilderness of the Chains, north west of Simonsbath. The steep sides of the Exmoor combes are clothed with woodland, mainly Sessile Oak, with Holly, Rowan, Whitethorn, Blackthorn, Hazel and ancient pollarded Ash trees. In some places, such as near the tiny church (said to be the smallest in Britain) in Culbone Woods, and around Watersmeet, there are rare species of whitebeams. Thanks to the high rainfall of the area, these woodlands contain many species of ferns, mosses, liverworts and lichens, and wildflowers such as Primrose, Stitchwort, Enchanter's Nightshade and Wood Anemone.

The damp valley bottom meadows provide a safe home for scarce wetland flowers, as well as butterflies, including three large fritillaries: the Dark Green, Silver Washed and the rare High Brown.

In spring, when the migrant birds return from Africa, these oak 'hangers' (which 'hang' on the valley sides) echo to the sound of Redstarts and a host of warblers: Garden Warblers, Blackcaps,

Above: *The Willow Warbler is the most numerous of all summer-visiting breeding birds to the British Isles.*

Right: *As in most parts of the British Isles, the Common Mole is abundant in grassland and woodland.*

Whitethroats, Willow and Wood Warblers and Chiffchaffs. Dapper little Pied Flycatchers often breed there too, encouraged by artificial nestboxes. Buzzards and Sparrowhawks use the taller trees for their bulky nests.

Fallow and Roe Deer live in the woods, and Red Deer use shelter there, though their chief home is on the open moor. Conspicuous in sunny glades are the huge nest mounds of Red Wood Ants.

The Barle is one of the loveliest rivers, with good populations of Atlantic Salmon and Brown Trout, as well as Dippers and Grey Wagtails and the rare Tree Lungwort Lichen on mature Ash trees. The ancient stone-slab clapper bridge at Tarr Steps beneath Winsford Hill is a mecca for tourists, but one can soon get away from the crowds.

Farmland and Coastline

The mosaic of farmland running onto the moorland provides habitats for a wide range of wildlife such as foxes, badgers, rabbits and moles and a variety of birds and insects. Some of the older hedges contain ten or more species of trees or shrubs, while old barns encourage declining Barn Owls to nest.

Sheep outnumber people by 50 to 1 here. Along with smaller numbers of beef cattle and horses, and the famous ponies, they graze the heather, tough grasses and tree seedlings, and help to maintain the open moorland landscape.

The northern boundary of the Park follows the coast for 54 kilometres (34 miles) from Combe

Martin in the west almost to Minehead in the east. The great rounded forms of the hog's-back coastal hills drop steeply to the sea: the cliffs include the highest in England at Great Hangman (244 metres/800 feet).

Some of the more exposed cliffs provide nesting sites for Fulmars, Kittiwakes, Guillemots, Razorbills, Jackdaws and Ravens, with a few pairs of Peregrine Falcons. The shoreline too is an exciting place, where one can explore pebble and shingle beaches, hidden inlets, and great caves that can be reached only by boat – or experienced rock climbers. The heavy rainfall running off the impermeable 'iron-pan' layer beneath the soil of the moors produces a torrential flow of water that has cut deep valleys into the coastal hills. The most devastating outcome of such erosion occurred in 1952 after an exceptionally wet summer, when the flooded River Lyn swept away part of the holiday town of Lynmouth; 34 people lost their lives.

Above: *The little harbour of Porlock Weir, once busy with trade and fishing, is now a popular base for sailing.*

Left: *A fine Red Deer stag roars a challenge to rivals in the rut.*

POOLE HARBOUR

The Dorset Heaths

Location: In Dorset, south coast of England, west of Bournemouth and south of Poole.

Climate: One of the sunniest, warmest parts of Britain in spring/summer, many fine days in autumn, can be misty and windy in winter; generally mild.

When to Go: Spring/summer best for flowers, insects and breeding birds; spring and autumn for bird migrants, including waders; winter for wildfowl and waders. Some areas very crowded in summer, so best to visit early morning or late in the day.

Access: By road via A351 from Bournemouth or Poole; for Arne go to Wareham then via minor road to Arne village for RSPB car park; for Studland continue to Corfe Castle and take B3351 to Studland village and toll road to reserve; or via ferry from Sandbanks. By rail to Bournemouth, Poole or (for Arne and Studland) Wareham, then local buses. Frequent boats to Brownsea Island from Poole Quay, Sandbanks and Bournemouth.

Permits: Brownsea Island: landing fee and charge for non-members of National Trust; restricted access to lagoon and hides for non-members of Dorset Wildlife Trust. Island open only 1 April–30 September.

Equipment: No special equipment required.

Facilities: RSPB hide at Arne; observation centre/hides by the Little Sea at Studland. Hides at lagoon on Brownsea, one with video link.

Watching Wildlife: Special heathland birds, butterflies, dragonflies, reptiles and plantlife.

Visitor Activities: Birdwatching, botany, entomology, walking, sailing.

With an area of over 3,500 hectares (8,700 acres), Poole Harbour is one of the largest natural harbours in the world, its waters bustling with ships of all sizes. To the east and north the shoreline is almost entirely swallowed by the town of Poole, together with many marinas, boat-building yards, potteries and other light industries. The western and southern shores, however, contain some of the most beautiful landscapes on the south coast, with internationally important lowland heather and gorse heathland, a precious remnant of the great Dorset heaths made famous by the writer Thomas Hardy. About 80 per cent of this mainly open habitat, unique to Western Europe, has been lost in Britain since 1800, when it was at its largest extent. The warm conditions in spring and summer enable plants and animals more characteristic of the Mediterranean to thrive. The area is at great risk from carelessly started fires.

Top left: *The Dorset heaths are among the last haunts of the Sand Lizard, rare in Britain.*

Opposite, top: *Looking across Poole Harbour from the woodland of Brownsea Island.*

Opposite, bottom left: *A jaunty male Dartford Warbler proclaims his territory from a gorse spray.*

Opposite, bottom centre: *A Sika doe: Sika were introduced to Britain from Japan in 1860.*

Opposite, bottom right: *A male Common Crossbill; this species occurs in the conifers on Brownsea Island*

ARNE RSPB RESERVE

Occupying 526 hectares (1,300 acres), this is owned and managed by the RSPB. The reserve's crowning glory is the extensive area of dry lowland heath, dominated by Heather, Bell Heather and Dwarf Gorse. There are also areas of mixed woodland, wet valley bogs and saltmarsh fringing Arne Bay.

Special Birds

Heathland birds here include two summer visitors: that beautiful falcon, the Hobby, dashing in hot pursuit of a dragonfly or small bird, and the Nightjar, which awakes at dusk, when the male reels out his strange churring song. A star attraction is the jaunty little Dartford Warbler, an essentially Mediterranean species on the edge of its range. It was almost wiped out in Britain by the cold weather of 1961–2 and 1962–3, but thanks to a run of mild winters it survived and increased its numbers and range. The best time to see this species is during the spring, when the males pour out their warbling songs from the tops of gorse bushes, but remember that these birds are vulnerable to disturbance. Other small birds include Stonechats and Linnets. In winter you may see a Hen Harrier gliding low over the ground, its long wings raised in a shallow 'V'.

The hide at Shipstal Point is a good place to view the waders and wildfowl on the mudflats of Poole Harbour, ideally an hour or so before high tide. As well as Oystercatchers, Ringed Plovers, Dunlins, Curlews and Redshanks, spring and autumn bring scarcer migrants, including Spotted Redshanks, Whimbrels and Greenshanks, while

Above: *The Royal Fern is one of Britain's most attractive ferns and thrives in boggy areas and moist acid woods in the Dorset heathlands.*

Below: *Brownsea Island was the first breeding site in Britain and Ireland for the Little Egret, steadily expanding its range.*

including 14 species of grasshoppers and crickets, and over 200 species of spider.

STUDLAND NNR

Owned and managed by the National Trust, this covers about 630 hectares (1,500 acres) and as well as a large area of heathland includes woodland, scrub, sphagnum bogs, freshwater, saltmarsh, sandy beaches and rare acidic sand dune habitat. Sheep's-bit, Common Centaury and other wild-flowers decorate the dunes stabilized with Marram Grass, while the wet slacks (damp areas between the dunes) hold Bog Myrtle, Royal Fern, Marsh Gentian and insectivorous sundews.

The dunes enclose a large freshwater lake called the Little Sea, attracting good numbers of wildfowl in winter, including Pintail, Goldeneye and Scaup, along with commoner species such as Mallard, Tufted Duck and Pochard. Other fine sites for wintering wildfowl and waders are Brand's Bay, a favourite site for Brent Geese, and looking out from the long curve of Studland Beach. Birds that can be seen out in Studland Bay in winter include Great Northern Divers, Great Crested, Slavonian and Black-necked Grebes, Wigeon and Eider. There is an impressive range of rare migrants, too.

In summer, the beach is very crowded: it has over a million visitors each year, and also contains Britain's largest naturist beach.

BROWNSEA ISLAND

Brownsea lies in the middle of Poole Harbour, between Poole and the Isle of Purbeck (which is part of the mainland), and is a haven for the naturalist.

nationally important numbers of Black-tailed Godwits build up by winter.

A Wealth of Wildlife

Arne, like Studland, is notable for being home to all six native British species of reptiles: the Adder, Grass Snake, Common Lizard and Slow-worm, and the rare Smooth Snake and Sand Lizard, all at the north-western limit of their breeding range.

Arne is a paradise for entomologists. No less than 33 species of butterfly have been recorded, including the lovely Silver-studded Blue on the heathland and the elegant White Admiral in the woods. Among the 22 species of dragonflies look out for the scarce Small Red Damselfly and the fast-flying Downy Emerald. Other insects abound,

The island also saw the beginning of the international Scout movement, when its founder, Robert (later Lord) Baden-Powell, held the first ever Boy Scout camp in 1907. Today, only Boy Scouts are allowed to camp there.

Although it covers only about 220 hectares (550 acres), being 1.6 kilometres (1 mile) long by 1.1 kilometres (¾ mile), it is by far the largest of several islands in Poole Harbour. It is owned by the National Trust, who lease the northern half to the Dorset Wildlife Trust as a 100-hectare (250-acre) nature reserve. It contains a surprising range of habitats, from lovely beaches, freshwaters and reedbeds to woodland and heathland.

Mixed woodland covers much of the island, with many Scots Pines and dense thickets of the invasive, introduced Rhododendron. This holds a range of small birds, including Wood Warblers and Crossbills.

Left: *The Smooth Snake, Britain's rarest snake, has its stronghold on the Dorset heaths.*

Productive Lagoon

The 25-hectare (62-acre) brackish-water lagoon, surrounded by reedbeds and saltmarsh, attracts many seabirds, wildfowl and waders. Seabirds include breeding Sandwich and Common Terns on artificial islands in summer. Many common waders can be seen, such as Oystercatchers, Curlews and Dunlin, as well as scarcer migrants, notably Greenshank and Spotted Redshank, in spring and autumn. Up to 700 graceful black-and-white Avocets visit in winter. Wildfowl include Shelduck and Wigeon, as well as scarcer species.

Tall trees surrounding the lagoon hold one of the largest heronries in Britain, with 70–100 noisy nesting pairs of Grey Herons in spring. Their smaller, dazzling white relatives, Little Egrets, which are in the process of colonizing Britain from the Continent, made the island famous by breeding there in 1996 – a first. At high tide, many of them roost in the lagoon trees; they can also be seen around the creeks and mudflats of Poole Harbour at high tide.

The island has at its centre a wet valley, with two lakes, reedbeds and wet alder and willow woodland (carr): these attract many small birds, including Sedge and Reed Warblers, as well as Water Rails.

Mammals include Red Squirrels at one of their few remaining sites in southern England, Water Voles and introduced Sika Deer.

Below: *Arne Nature Reserve, established by the RSPB in 1965, includes fine woodland as well as major remnants of heathland.*

SOUTH/CENTRAL ENGLAND

THIS LARGE AREA, OCCUPYING 47,000 square kilometres (18,150 square miles), includes the counties of Hampshire and Gloucestershire in the south west, Sussex and Kent in the south east, and Shropshire and Leicestershire further north. The multitude of uses to which this land has been put over the centuries has produced a mosaic of habitats, from medieval hunting forests to plantations of alien conifers, and from rolling downland and ancient lowland heaths to arable farmland and great reservoirs supplying the dense population.

There are many towns and cities, yet despite this wild places abound. Even in the huge

urban sprawl of London rural pockets such as Epping Forest and Wimbledon Common contain a surprising variety of plants and animals.

Only an hour from London lie the rolling North and South Downs, with protected remnants of ancient wildflower- and insect-rich grassland. Further north are the chalk ridge of the Chilterns and the limestone escarpment of the Cotswolds, with its picture-book villages. Such places make great walking country.

The area also includes wetland and coastal sites, such as Slimbridge, renowned for wildfowl, and the huge shingle expanse of Dungeness, with its rare migrant birds and insects and special flowers.

Although winters can be cold, there is sunny, warm weather in summer and, with East Anglia, south-eastern England is the driest part of the British Isles. This, and proximity to the Continent, creates suitable conditions for various animals and plants at the northern limit of their distribution, and the first landing sites for migrants from Europe and Africa. Aided by the recent warming of the climate, some species, such as the Mediterranean Gull, have begun their British colonization here.

Opposite, left: *The dull scarlet Yew berry. Southern England boasts some of the finest Yew woodlands in Britain.*

Below: *A tranquil scene at Cuckmere Haven, where the River Cuckmere meanders through the soft chalk of the South Downs, cutting off oxbow lakes in the process. This is one of a number of areas of the downs renowned for their wildflowers.*

SLIMBRIDGE

Wildfowl Haven

Location: On the River Severn, in Gloucestershire, 16 km (10 miles) from Gloucester.

Climate: Can be wet or foggy in winter.

When to Go: Most people visit Slimbridge in late summer, but winter is the best time for birdwatching.

Access: By road, turn off M5 (from north, take Junction 13; from south, Junction 14), along A38 and onto a minor road for Slimbridge village and reserve. By train from Bristol or Gloucester to Cam & Dursley, then taxi.

Permits: None required. Entry fee for non-members of WWT.

Equipment: No special equipment required.

Facilities: Award-winning Discovery Centre, Observation Tower. To avoid disturbance to the wild birds, screened walkways lead from the centre to a series of hides.

Watching Wildlife: Two major attractions are the largest wintering flocks of White-fronted Geese in Britain, and several hundred Bewick's Swans. Wildfowl (captive as well as wild), and other wild birds including waders and birds of prey, and a selection of water and damp-loving plants: Marsh Marigolds (Kingcups), Purple Loosestrife, and Teasel, which attracts flocks of Goldfinches. Mammals include Water Voles along the lake shores, nationally becoming ever rarer as their bankside habitat is altered.

Visitor Activities: Birdwatching and other natural history pursuits; good place to take children.

Slimbridge Wildfowl & Wetlands Trust Centre, on the upper reaches of the River Severn, was founded as the Severn Wildfowl Trust in 1946 by the great naturalist Sir Peter Scott. He visited the area in search of the Lesser White-fronted Goose, a rare wanderer to Western Europe from the Arctic, and only officially recorded once in Britain. He found two more, and decided that Slimbridge would be the ideal place for the research station he had long been planning. In 1955 Slimbridge became the headquarters of the Wildfowl Trust. Renamed in 1989 as the Wildfowl & Wetlands Trust (WWT), it has eight other centres in the British Isles, including the remarkable Wetland Centre in London, Europe's largest urban wetland creation project.

Slimbridge protects about 500 hectares (1,235 acres): great expanses of mudflats, saltmarsh, lagoons and grazing meadows, which hold nationally important numbers of wildfowl and waders in winter. It has been designated a Ramsar Site and

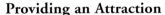

Top left: A Mute Swan investigates the camera.

Opposite, top: View across South Lake.

Opposite, bottom left: White-fronted Geese can be seen between late October and early March.

Opposite, bottom right: Each Bewick's Swan can be identified by the unique pattern on its bill.

SPA and an SSSI. It also contains the largest and most comprehensive collection of wildfowl (swans, geese and ducks) – and flamingos – in the world.

The great expanse of the Dumbles grazing saltmarsh was created centuries ago inside the sea walls that hold back the Severn. The same process produced the even larger area known as the New Grounds. The careful management of the water table ensures that these special grasslands remain wet throughout winter.

Pools, lakes, shallow watery scrapes and reedbeds have been created. Artificial floating islands attract Common Terns, and the first two chicks were reared in 2000. Blackthorn and Hawthorn hedges provide cover and food for migrant passerines such as Redwings and Fieldfares.

Providing an Attraction

Sir Peter Scott set out the three aims of the Trust as conservation, research and education, and this continues to form the basis of WWT's work today, with the addition of a fourth aim in 1982: recreation and entertainment. The site has been extensively redeveloped, and the new centre buildings were opened during 2000.

An Abundance of Bird Life

Slimbridge is a major wintering site for White-fronted Geese that breed on the Siberian tundra. On average 1,500 birds gather here, often with an increase in late February before migrating to their

Right: The award-winning Discovery Centre includes a cinema, restaurant, shop and wildlife art gallery. The Observation Tower (background) gives stunning bird's-eye views of goose flocks flying across the reserve.

Below: Feeding the wildfowl on Swan Lake, Slimbridge.

breeding grounds. Colder weather on the Continent can bring over 5,000 birds to Slimbridge, but milder winters and improved protection have resulted in greater numbers only migrating as far as Germany and the Netherlands.

The flocks often contain members of other goose species, either escapees (though not usually from Slimbridge) or local feral Greylag, Barnacle or Canada Geese, or wild Pink-footed, Bean and Brent Geese, and sometimes one of the rare Lesser White-fronts.

Several hundred Bewick's Swans grace Slimbridge each autumn after flying some 4,000 kilometres (2,500 miles) from breeding areas in Arctic Russia. Most graze on the wet grasslands by day, but towards dusk fly in to Swan Lake and Rushy Pen. This great spectacle can be enjoyed from the comfortable Peng Observatory.

Large numbers of ducks visit Slimbridge, especially in winter. Most abundant are Wigeon, Teal, Mallard, Pochard, Tufted Duck and Gadwall, with increasing numbers of Pintail. Some enter the wildfowl enclosures and become almost as tame as the captive birds.

Huge flocks of gulls roost on the estuary in winter, with over 10,000 Black-headed and Common Gulls possible. Winter waders include up to 10,000 Lapwings, 5,000 Dunlin, 900 Golden Plover and 600 Curlews.

Birds of prey include Sparrowhawks, Kestrels, Merlins, and especially Peregrines; Little Owls can often be seen in broad daylight. Slimbridge is one of the best places in Britain for Water Rails: these secretive birds are attracted to the feeding stations during hard weather. Kingfishers are regularly seen and sometimes nest.

Research Work

The marking of wildfowl with lightweight coded rings was carried out here from the earliest days. A renovated decoy and a cage trap are used to catch the birds for ringing, at the same time recording their measurements, weight and age. Analysis of the data enables scientists to learn about their movements, survival rates and breeding biology. The use of plastic leg rings was developed at Slimbridge in the late 1960s by Dr Malcolm Ogilvie. Engraved with bigger letters, they can be read using binoculars or telescopes, so removing the need for trapping.

An additional method of tracking individual birds is used for Bewick's Swans; each has a different pattern on the bill, and drawings of these, started by Sir Peter and his daughter Dafila, have produced a register. Bewick's Swans are usually monogamous and each brood of up to five cygnets stays with their parents throughout their first winter. They tend to be faithful to their wintering sites, and several individuals have returned to Slimbridge for almost 30 years.

Captive Breeding Programmes

WWT's greatest conservation success story has been the rescue of the Hawaiian Goose, or Nene, from extinction. Captive breeding and research at Slimbridge and subsequent reintroduction to Hawaii saved this attractive bird, whose world population was down to only 20–30 in 1949. Work also goes on to help save rare species of ducks facing extinction, such as the Baikal Teal from eastern Asia, and Laysan Duck from Hawaii.

Slimbridge is also a world leader in the conservation of flamingos. These elegant birds face threats worldwide and need all the help they can get.

THE SOUTH DOWNS

Chalk Grassland and Sea Views

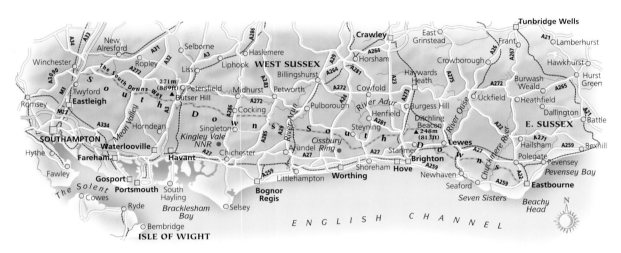

The South Downs comprises 1,375 square kilometres (503 square miles) of low, rolling chalk hills. The name 'downs' comes from the Celtic word *dun*, a 'fort' or 'hill'. The downs afford sweeping panoramas: to the north, the chequerboard farmland and woodland of the undulating Weald; to the south, as far as the English Channel.

The area is an AONB, and is likely to be awarded National Park status in the near future. The South Downs include some fine walking country less than two hours from London; there are an estimated 32 million visits each year, more than to any of the existing National Parks.

Plants, Insects and Birds

Chalk downland is one of the richest wildflower habitats in the British Isles, with over 300 species in the South Downs, including the wild aromatic herbs Thyme, Marjoram and Basil, and delicate blue Harebells, with specialities such as Squinancywort, Round-headed Rampion and a variety of orchids.

The dark green 'fairy rings' that appear on the turf result from fungi spreading outwards from a central point; some of the larger examples are

Top right: *The dramatic chalk cliffs of Beachy Head at the eastern end of the South Downs.*

centuries old. There is a rich variety of butterflies, grasshoppers and bush crickets, and nationally scarce glow-worms (carnivorous beetles) can be found.

The open landscape suits Red-legged and Grey Partridges, Skylarks and Yellowhammers. Spring and autumn brings migrant birds to the downs, including many Wheatears. These were once trapped by shepherds, who supplemented their income by selling them in London. In winter, as well as flocks of Lapwings, you may spot a handsome Great Grey Shrike, a scarce visitor from the continent.

Woodland

Broad-leaved woodland, typically Beech, clothes the flattish tops (where clay, flint and a deep layer of rich soil overly the chalk) and the chalky slopes, together with Oak and other trees. To the west of the River Arun lie plantations of conifers and mixed trees as well as natural broadleaved woods; the Meon valley is particularly attractive.

In the beautiful chalk valley of Kingley Vale near Chichester is a great natural Yew wood, said to be the finest in Europe. The biggest Yews stand at the foot of the valley; many are thought to be over 500 years old. One of the first National Nature Reserves, established in 1952, Kingley Vale is rich in birdlife, including Wrens, Robins, Blackbirds,

Location: Extends for 160 km (99 miles) from Beacon Hill, near Winchester, Hampshire, to end at the sheer chalk cliffs of Beachy Head, just east of Eastbourne, East Sussex.

Climate: Can be very warm and sunny from spring to autumn, especially in sheltered valleys, but often windy on the tops; winter brings more rain, mist and occasional snow.

When to Go: Spring, summer and early autumn are best for wild-flowers, butterflies and insects. Winter can be bleak, with little evident wildlife, although some areas hold interesting birds, including Lapwings, Skylarks, Linnets and Hen Harriers and, in a few places, Great Grey Shrikes.

Access: By road, via local roads from M3 for the Hampshire side of downs and M/A23 for Sussex side. By train from London to various stations; many bus routes cross the downs.

Permits: None required.

Equipment: No special equipment required.

Facilities: Few on the downs themselves, but many attractive villages nestle in the valleys and to north and south, and larger towns such as Chichester are within a short distance. The 161-km (100-mile) South Downs Way affords superb views in all directions on clear days, and uniquely allows horse riders and cyclists as well as ramblers. Weald and Downland Open Air Museum, Cocking, West Sussex.

Watching Wildlife: A wealth of special flowers and insects.

Visitor Activities: Walking, archaeology, botany, entomology (especially butterfly-watching), birdwatching; cycling, horse riding, hang-gliding, kite flying, angling.

Top: *Ancient Yew trees form living sculptures at Kingley Vale NNR in Sussex.*

Above: *Pyramidal Orchids and a host of other wildflowers flourish in unimproved chalk grassland on the South Downs in July.*

Goldcrests and other breeding species. In autumn and winter, yew and hawthorn berries attract large numbers of thrushes, finches and tits. It is also home to Roe and Fallow Deer, Badgers and Stoats.

The Effects of Man

Open downland results from a long period of human intervention. Originally clothed with forest, the downs were gradually cleared by prehistoric farmers. Sheep rearing began during the medieval period and reached its peak just before the Industrial Revolution in the mid-18th century, creating the characteristic springy turf and allowing wildflowers to flourish; the region gave its name to the famous Southdown sheep in the 19th century. From the 18th century deliberately released rabbits grazed the downs and helped to maintain this artificial but wildlife-rich habitat.

Today, much of the chalk grassland has been ploughed up and great, prairie-like arable fields have replaced the sheep. Rabbits, too, declined after the introduction of myxomatosis in 1953. The application of fertilizers to create 'improved grassland' has choked out most of the wildflowers. Afforestation too has altered the landscape. In the early 19th century about half the South Downs was covered with unimproved chalk grassland; only 5 per cent or so remains.

But there are still areas of untouched downland. Chalk grassland is a scarce habitat internationally, and the South Downs have recently been declared an ESA. This has encouraged some farmers to return arable areas to grazing livestock, and to manage field margins less intensively to maximize wildlife.

Old downland is characterized by the many small hummocks of soil, covered by grasses or other plants such as Thyme, that are the nest mounds of Yellow Meadow Ants. They indicate that an area has not been ploughed for many years, probably centuries. Red Ants and Black Ants are also found, and protect the caterpillars of the Adonis Blue and the Chalkhill Blue butterflies from predators.

Rivers and Dewponds

There are few streams, and many dry wooded valleys where rivers once ran. Several broad river valleys do still cut through the area: the Meon, Arun, Adur, Ouse and Cuckmere. The watercourses are home to many freshwater animals, including dragonflies, damselflies and White-clawed Crayfish, the only crayfish species native to the British Isles.

Dewponds – small, rounded ponds high on the downs – were once thought to be of prehistoric origin, but are now considered no more than 200 years old. About a metre (3 feet) deep, they were filled by rain, mist and run-off, providing water for sheep and oases for aquatic wildlife. Professional dewpond makers worked as recently as 1939.

The South Downs Way

This long-distance path (161 kilometres/100 miles) follows the undulating crest of the downs. It begins in the historic cathedral town of Winchester (a major Roman settlement, and England's capital city in the early 9th century AD) and runs east to dramatic Beachy Head, rising 135 metres (443 feet) above the waves. Although parts of the route are steep, there are no lengthy climbs; Butser Hill (271 metres/889 feet) near Petersfield is the highest point on the downs. On its slopes is a fine reconstruction of a Celtic farm.

Other places worth a visit include the Weald and Downland Open Air Museum, Cocking, where you can see a range of traditional rural crafts. To the east, Chanctonbury Ring (238 metres/783 feet) was named after the circle of Beech trees planted in 1760 by a local landowner. Many were destroyed by the major storm of 1987, but this revealed the remains of an Iron Age hillfort and a Roman temple. Just south of this lies Cissbury, the second largest Iron Age fort in England.

Above: *A view across the splendid downland near Beachy Head, Sussex. This is one of the best parts of the South Downs for botanists, with rare plants including Early Spider Orchid and Burnt Orchid.*

Left: *Among the glories of the South Downs are several species of blue butterflies: this is the Chalkhill Blue.*

THE NEW FOREST

Ancient Stronghold of Special Wildlife

Location: In Hampshire, between Southampton and Bournemouth, with small town of Lyndhurst at its centre.

Climate: Often warm and sunny from spring to autumn, winter can bring rain, mist and cold.

When to Go: Spring and summer bring the greatest variety of wildlife, including reptiles. May–June especially good for breeding birds, and June–August for butterflies and dragonflies.

Access: By road via M3 and M27 to Cadnam, and A337 to Lyndhurst and Brockenhurst, and on minor roads to different sites within the Forest; by rail, main line to Southampton, then local services to Ashurst, Beaulieu Road, Brockenhurst and Lymington; also buses and taxis.

Permits: None required.

Equipment: No special equipment required.

Facilities: New Forest museum and visitor centre at Lyndhurst; New Forest Otter, Owl and Wildlife Park at Longdown; National Motor Museum at Beaulieu; Maritime Museum at Buckler's Hard. Forestry Commission provides many picnic and camping sites, and guided walks.

Watching Wildlife: Renowned for its ancient trees and wealth of insects, reptiles, birds, deer and other mammals; also superb for fungi, lichens, mosses, liverworts, and some special wildflowers.

Visitor Activities: Birdwatching, entomology, botany and other wildlife interests, walking, cycling, sailing and other watersports as well as diving on coast. Very good for families, with easy walking, plenty of picnic sights and varied attractions, from pony trekking to a variety of museums.

Occupying an area of about 580 square kilometres (224 square miles) in south-west Hampshire, the New Forest is a mosaic of woodland, bogland and grass and heather heathland, surrounded by farmland. The largest area of uncultivated land in lowland England, and one of the most important areas of ancient lowland forest in North-western Europe, it contains some of the richest communities of wildlife in the British Isles.

The name seems somewhat inappropriate, since large areas are unforested and it is certainly not new. It dates from AD1079, when William the Conqueror decreed the area to be a Royal hunting reserve for the protection of venison (deer meat) and vert (the right to cut green wood) for his exclusive use. Severe penalties, including death, were meted out to anyone bold enough to trespass in the Forest or harm the deer, wild boar or wolves.

With the decline of deer hunting, the Forest became increasingly important as a source of timber, particularly during the Napoleonic Wars in the late 18th and early 19th centuries, when huge quantities of oak were ferried downriver to Royal Navy shipyards at Buckler's Hard, Gosport and Portsmouth.

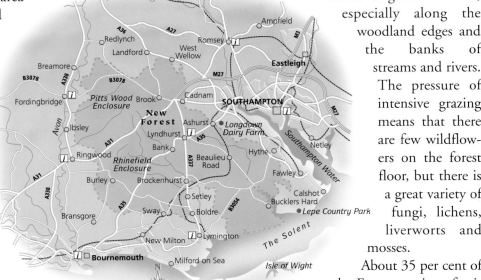

Top left: *In Britain found only in the New Forest, the Wild Gladiolus flowers in June and July.*

Opposite: *A winter scene in the New Forest.*

The main trees are old Oak and Beech in the most mature forest, with Birch, Ash, Scots Pine, Hawthorn and other species; the understorey is mainly Holly. Intensive grazing by livestock produces the typical close-cropped 'lawns' of grass and moss, especially along the woodland edges and the banks of streams and rivers. The pressure of intensive grazing means that there are few wildflowers on the forest floor, but there is a great variety of fungi, lichens, liverworts and mosses.

About 35 per cent of the Forest consists of privately owned unenclosed grazing land; the rest is owned by the Crown, and managed by the Forestry Commission for timber production, with much fenced off as 'inclosures' to protect the young trees from deer.

Attractive villages are dotted around the Forest – including Lyndhurst with its New Forest museum and visitor centre – and these provide good bases for exploration. The Forest is protected as a Heritage Area, but will be designated a National Park in the near future.

Special Insects

There is a rich variety of butterflies and moths, and in the many wetland areas dragonflies and damselflies include two species more characteristic of the Mediterranean, the Scarce Blue-tailed Damselfly and the Small Red Damselfly.

Above: *Sporting an impressive pair of antler-shaped jaws, the male Stag Beetle is aptly named. He uses these in ritual jousting contests with rival males.*

Below: *A New Forest Pony.*

More species of beetles have been recorded here than in any other part of the British Isles. The most dramatic is the Stag Beetle, the largest of all British land insects at over 5 centimetres (2 inches) long for males. A speciality in sunny glades is the New Forest Cicada, the only species of cicada native to the British Isles. Its song is of such high frequency that many people cannot hear it. Grasshoppers and bush crickets are also well represented, including the largest British grasshopper, the Large Marsh Grasshopper, which can be found in areas of floating bog. You may also hear the purring songs of Wood Crickets, flightless true crickets, in the woods.

After wet weather, puddles may be full of little Fairy Shrimps, hatched from eggs laid in dusty hollows that are filled with water only after heavy rain.

New Forest Birdlife

The New Forest is rich in birdlife, and a springtime visit will guarantee a truly impressive dawn chorus. The variety of habitat, with trees of all ages and many left to decay rather than being removed, provides plenty of rotting wood from which nest holes can be excavated and insect grubs dug out.

Among the many breeding species in the woodlands there are Wood Warblers, Redstarts and all three British species of woodpeckers: the scarcest, the little Lesser Spotted Woodpecker, feeds high in the canopy. Hawfinches breed, too, but are most easily seen in late autumn and winter when they feed on the ground or return to communal roosts. Among conifers are small numbers of Firecrests and Crossbills. Woodland predators include Kestrels and Tawny Owls, as well as Honey Buzzards, rare in Britain.

The open heaths are home to Stonechats and Dartford Warblers. The area also has a thriving Hobby population, and these dashing falcons can be seen above the heaths and bogs hunting insects and small birds. Where woodland borders heath there are Nightjars, Woodlarks and Tree Pipits, while the valley bogs and marshes hold breeding Lapwing, Curlew, Snipe and Redshank.

Reptiles and Mammals

The dry sandy soils and warm summer climate make the heathlands attractive to all six of the British Isles' native reptile species, including rare Smooth Snakes and Sand Lizards. Thanks to the many boggy areas, flooded pits, ponds and streams, there are good populations of Common and Great Crested Newts, Common Frogs and Common Toads.

The Forest holds four deer species: Red, Roe, Fallow and Sika. You are most likely to see Fallow Deer, the most numerous, as they emerge cautiously from the woods to graze. Sika, descendants of escapees from the Beaulieu estate, prefer to hide among dense cover of the younger, mostly coniferous, woodland.

There are also good populations of Badgers, Foxes and other mammals. Like the reptiles, they are generally elusive and most are nocturnal. Hollows in the ancient decaying trees provide roost sites for 13 of the 16 British bat species.

Traditional Management

The forest is still run largely on ancient lines. About 350 Forest families are Commoners, granted grazing rights by virtue of owning land or other property. Few still make a living from stock-keeping; most supplement their income by other work, and some keep one or two animals to maintain the old traditions.

Ancient Commoners' rights include the no-longer-exercised Commons of Turbary (the right to cut peat for house fires) and Estovers (the right to cut wood for fuel), as well as Pasture, or grazing rights. There are ten Verderers, five elected by the Commoners and five appointed by official bodies. They are the guardians of the Forest, working with the Forestry Commission to balance the Commoners' needs for grazing with the requirements of conservation and amenity use. In turn, the Verderers appoint five Agisters, who deal with the day-to-day management and welfare of the Commoners' livestock. Twelve Keepers, today appointed by the Forestry Commission, undertake a range of duties concerning wildlife, conservation and recreation.

There are over 3,000 semi-wild New Forest Ponies, a small, hardy breed that may be any colour except piebald and skewbald. The Agisters organize an annual round-up (or 'drift') to count them, brand them with their owners' marks, and check their condition before the winter. Cattle, sheep, pigs and donkeys are also turned out to graze.

Left: *A Great Spotted Woodpecker pauses in its ascent of a mossy, decaying tree trunk.*

Below: *A well-antlered adult male, or buck, Fallow Deer, and a young male stop to sniff the breeze in a New Forest clearing.*

DUNGENESS

One of Europe's Largest Shingle Beaches

Location: Extreme south-eastern corner of England, protruding into the English Channel 5 km (3 miles) south east of Lydd, Kent.

Climate: Can be bleak, swept by winds and shrouded in fog, especially in autumn and winter; summer often brings very warm, sunny weather.

When to Go: Spring and summer for breeding birds, wildflowers and amphibians; spring and autumn for bird and insect migrants; winter brings wildfowl, grebes and divers.

Access: By several minor roads south from the A259. By rail to Rye (16 km/10 miles away) or Folkestone (25 km/16 miles), then local bus route 12 from Folkestone or Lydd, or taxi. From Easter–September daily, and on Saturdays and Sundays in March and October, you can use the miniature steam trains of the Romney, Hythe & Dymchurch Railway (Hythe to Dungeness).

Permits: None required; avoid private roads.

Equipment: Waterproofs in winter.

Facilities: Visitor centre and shop at RSPB Nature Reserve; circular trail and 6 hides; Dungeness Bird Observatory has basic self-catering accommodation for up to 10 birdwatchers, bookable via warden, 01797 321309 or email dungeness.obs@tinyonline.co.uk

Watching Wildlife: Dungeness is renowned as one of the best places in Britain for observing bird – and insect – migration. It has one of south-east England's largest breeding colonies of gulls and terns on RSPB reserve.

Visitor Activities: Birdwatching, entomology, botany.

Jutting out into the English Channel, Dungeness can be bleak and lonely, often windswept and fog-bound, but it has a unique beauty and an impressive range of wildlife and plants.

Dungeness is an 'apposition' type of beach, in which new shingle is continually deposited on the flank of an earlier beach. It accumulates until a particularly high tide lifts it out of reach of further tides, and a new beach starts to form. Over about 4,000 years this has produced a succession of roughly parallel ridges. The sea also constantly moves pebbles from the south-west-facing side round the tip of the foreland to the east side, so that the foreland is travelling slowly eastwards. Recently this has been counteracted by excavating shingle on the eastern side and dumping it back where it came from.

Dungeness is a complex mosaic of bare pebbles, typical shoreline shingle plants and, where the pebbles are stable, large expanses of grasses and wind-stunted Sallow, Elder, Gorse and Bramble scrub, frequently

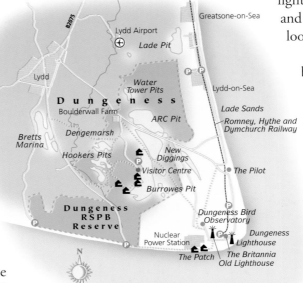

Top left: *A fine male Whinchat, one of Dungeness' migrant songbirds, in breeding plumage.*

Opposite, top: *Fishing boats on the shingle.*

Opposite, bottom left: *A stunning drake Smew.*

Opposite, bottom right: *The Mediterranean Gull breeds in small but increasing numbers here.*

interspersed with pools and the occasional clump of buildings, abandoned automobiles and other junk. Looming out of this strange landscape are two massive nuclear power stations, towering over the little fishermen's cottages and disused lighthouses, while power lines and pylons serve as useful lookout posts for Kestrels.

Nicknamed 'Dunge' by birdwatchers, Dungeness is a great place to see a wide variety of birds. The outflow of warm water from the reactors – known as 'the Patch' – attracts gulls, terns and other seabirds. For decades, the solitude of Dungeness was shattered by the noise of gravel-extraction machinery, but today many of the workings are abandoned and flooded, providing a welcoming refuge for waterbirds.

The Dungeness RSPB Nature Reserve – the Society's first, established in 1931 – occupies about 485 hectares (1,200 acres). As well as being able to explore the habitat on a circular trail, you can watch birds in comfort from the hides or from the visitor centre. The Dungeness Bird Observatory, founded in 1952, has basic accommodation for birdwatchers.

Breeding Birds

Over 60 breeding species have been recorded, 40-45 usually nesting in any one year. The gravel-pit islands provide safe havens for nesting seabirds, including Common and Sandwich Terns, and a few pairs of Common Gulls, the latter at one of their few regular breeding sites in England. Small but

Above: *Sea Kale in bloom brightens up the almost lunar landscape at Dungeness, with the nuclear power station and one of the lighthouses in the background.*

increasing numbers of truly black-hooded Mediterranean Gulls nest among large colonies of Black-headed Gulls, which have dark chocolate-brown half-hoods in the breeding season.

Other breeders among the scrub and shingle include Red-legged Partridges, Yellowhammers and Corn Buntings, the last having declined massively in most parts of the British Isles recently. Scarce Black Redstarts sometimes nest around the power station.

Migrant Birds and Insect Wanderers
Dungeness is renowned as one of the best places for observing bird migration. Spring brings the greatest variety of offshore migrants, including divers, Brent Geese, seaducks, and also waders, skuas, gulls, terns and auks. Dungeness is the most reliable site in Britain for seeing migrating Pomarine Skuas, with peak numbers in early May. Numbers and variety are less in autumn, though gales may blow Manx and Sooty Shearwaters, Leach's Petrels or Sabine's Gulls within range of birdwatchers.

The area provides a first landfall for exhausted migrant landbirds from across the Channel in spring, or a last resting stop before departing in autumn. Given the right weather – south-easterly winds with overcast skies or rain – 'falls' of large numbers of migrant passerines can be forced to land. As well as many Willow Warblers, Whitethroats and other common warblers, Whinchats and other chats and Spotted and Pied Flycatchers, these can include scarcities such as Hoopoes, Wrynecks, Bluethroats, Red-backed Shrikes and Golden Orioles, with the chance of rare warblers in autumn.

Right: *Romney Marsh has a lonely beauty with its great expanses of reclaimed farmland beneath huge skies, as here looking towards Fairfield Church.*

Autumn also brings flocks of finches and thrushes from Northern and Eastern Europe: Chaffinches, Redwings and Fieldfares. Scarcer visitors include tiny Firecrests. As winter draws in, Hen Harriers and Merlins visit the area, on the lookout for small birds.

As well as commoner species such as feral Canada Geese, Pochard and Tufted Duck, winter wildfowl on the flooded gravel pits include Goldeneye, Smew from Scandinavia and Russia, and Ruddy Duck. Bewick's Swans from Russia sometimes roost on the water after feeding on nearby Romney Marsh. The gravel pits also attract a few Red-necked or Black-necked Grebes, blown in from the sea, as well as the more numerous resident Great Crested Grebes.

Various species of dragonflies and damselflies also wander in or are blown across the Channel. Migrant butterflies – Peacock, Red Admiral, Clouded Yellow and Painted Lady – can sometimes be seen in great numbers, as well as occasional much rarer visitors, such as Pale Clouded Yellows or Monarchs. Breeding butterflies include scarce Essex Skippers as well as common Gatekeepers and Small Coppers. Many unusual migrant moths have been recorded in late summer and autumn, including striking hawk moths, while breeding species include the nationally rare

Pygmy Footman and Scarce Chocolate-tip, the latter breeding nowhere else in the British Isles, as well as day-flying Cinnabar and Six-spot Burnet moths.

Special Plantlife

Despite the tough conditions, many unusual wild-flowers can be found. Looking like overgrown cauli-flowers when in flower on the shingle, great clumps of Sea Kale form some of the largest populations of what is now a scarce plant nationally. The young shoots were greatly valued as a local culinary delicacy.

Other scarce wildflowers include Marsh Cinque-foil, Yellow Vetch, Nottingham Catchfly, Upright Chickweed and Bulbous Meadow-grass. Holmstone Wood is a unique wood of stunted Holly trees, documented as long ago as the 8th century.

Romney Marsh

The foreland encloses the region known as Romney Marsh (consisting of Romney and Welland Marshes). In Roman times Dungeness was a partly submerged sandbank, and the settlements of Lydd and Old Romney, now well inland, were on the edge of Romney Bay. As the sea level fell over the centuries, marshland developed, and much land was reclaimed.

Left: *Migrant insects regularly recorded at Dungeness include the impressive Migrant Hawker dragonfly: this one is a male.*

Although much of the ancient damp pasture has been replaced by deep-drained arable fields, Romney Marsh still retains areas where the famous Romney Marsh sheep graze. In winter, flocks of Golden Plover and Lapwings wheel and turn in the huge open skies or gather on the pastures. Woodland around the marsh attracts good numbers of Nightingales to breed, arriving from Africa in spring.

The loud croaking love calls of male Marsh Frogs are one of the most distinctive sounds in April and May. These large amphibians are not natives, but were introduced from Hungary in 1934–5 to a local garden pond.

EAST ANGLIA

DURING THE MIDDLE AGES, EAST ANGLIA WAS A SAXON KINGDOM, covering the counties of Norfolk, Suffolk and part of Cambridgeshire. Today many would include the whole of Cambridgeshire, and some would also add part of Essex: on this basis the region covers 14,405 square kilometres (5,562 square miles).

East Anglia forms a great bulge of land extending out into the North Sea. Originally a vast malaria-ridden swamp, much of it was drained for growing crops in the rich black peaty soil, and is still known as Fenland. Only a few remnants of the original fens are left,

such as the National Trust's Wicken Fen, Britain's first Nature Reserve, home to a wide range of water-loving plants, insects and animals, smaller fragments at Woodwalton and Holme Fens, and the Ouse Washes, famed for its huge concentrations of waterbirds, especially Bewick's Swans.

Although much of the area is now given over to great hedgeless fields of wheat, barley, sugarbeet and oilseed rape, there are oases of more varied and wildlife-rich habitats, such as the remarkable landscape of Breckland (the nearest habitat in the British Isles to steppeland), and the Norfolk Broads, popular with tourists and naturalists alike.

The coastline is generally wild and unspoilt, with extensive mudflats, saltmarshes, sandy and shingle beaches and dunes, and internationally renowned for its birdlife. Much of it is protected in a chain of reserves, including those at Cley, Titchwell and Minsmere. The Wash, in the far north-east, is one of Europe's finest estuaries, with huge numbers of waders in winter and a thriving population of Common Seals.

Opposite, top: *The once common Water Vole is now a rare sight along Britain's banks.*

Below: *The attractive village of Cley, on the north Norfolk coast, is renowned among birders for the nature reserve at Cley Marshes, lying just to its east. Attracting a huge range of birds, it is arguably Britain's premier birding site.*

THE OUSE WASHES

Traditionally Managed Wetlands

The largest area of regularly flooded meadowland in Britain, the Ouse Washes is internationally important for its vast numbers of winter wildfowl. The 2,500-hectare (6,250-acre) strip is a Ramsar site, and almost three-quarters is owned or managed by the RSPB, WWT and The Wildlife Trusts, protecting a vital remnant of a habitat that has almost disappeared from Britain. Most of it is fields with ditches, pools and willow beds; 'Washes' refers to the fields, flooded in winter.

Fenland History

This is one of the few small remaining parts of what was once a vast area of flat, low-lying fenland, covering some 6,350 square kilometres (2,450 square miles) from just north of Cambridge east to King's Lynn in Norfolk and north to Boston in Lincolnshire.

Known as 'The Fens' or 'Fenland', for centuries this was a wild, desolate region, subject to seasonal flooding. The only human inhabitants were the small, tough communities of 'fen tigers' who eked

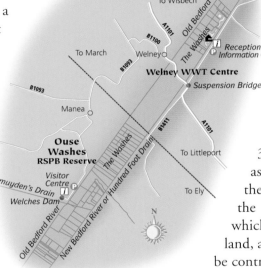

Top left: *A Common Frog peers out from a carpet of duckweed. Carefully managed sites such as the Ouse Washes are important for increasingly threatened populations of Britain's amphibians.*

Opposite, top: *Welches Dam.*

Opposite, bottom: *Birdwatching from a hide at Welney Wildfowl & Wetland Trust Centre.*

out a damp, lonely existence, cutting peat for fuel and surviving largely on fish and wildfowl.

Then in 1634 the great Dutch engineer Cornelius Vermuyden was commissioned by the fourth Earl of Bedford to plan and supervise the draining of large areas of The Fens to produce farmland. This involved digging out artificial waterways, first the Old Bedford river and later, in 1651, the parallel New Bedford river. Only 1 kilometre (0.6 miles) apart, the canals extended north eastwards from Earith for about 32 kilometres (20 miles). Straight as a ruler for much of their length, these huge drains took water from the meandering Great Ouse river, which regularly flooded vast areas of land, and so enabled the water levels to be controlled for the first time.

An unfortunate side effect of this impressive engineering feat was that the peat dried out and the level of the farmland dropped below that of the rivers, eventually by several metres. The remedy was to use windmill-driven pumps, then steam-driven, and finally diesel and electric pumps, to drain the land.

Traditional Management

Almost all The Fens have long been converted into the richest agricultural land. However, this is still a remote and isolated landscape of great, flat, hedgeless, black fields, separated by drainage ditches and stretching endlessly to the horizon under a vast sky.

In contrast to the rest of Fenland, the Ouse Washes have been managed in the same way for hundreds of years, grazed by cattle or cut for hay in summer and allowed to flood in winter. The reserves

Above: *Whooper Swans start to fly in from their Icelandic breeding grounds to winter on the Ouse Washes in early October; numbers reach a peak in mid-January. They leave later than Bewick's Swans, with some lingering until early April.*

the Siberian tundra, with over 4,500 birds – almost half the British wintering population – at peak times. They can be seen most easily at Welney, where after dark they are artificially fed, and can be watched from the comfort of a heated observatory.

Ducks throng to the Ouse Washes in far greater numbers, with almost 30,000 Wigeon most winters, as well as Pochard, Mallard, Pintail and Shoveler.

Winter brings Hen Harriers and Short-eared Owls, searching for bird or small mammal prey. Little Owls and Barn Owls are residents, nesting in hollows in old willow trees, as do Stock Doves.

Visiting migrants in spring and autumn include a great variety of waders: Green and Wood Sandpipers, Little Stints and Curlew Sandpipers, and up to 1,800 Black-tailed Godwits of the race breeding in Iceland, with redder breasts than the European race, which breeds here in small but increasing numbers. You may be lucky enough to witness an extraordinary early morning courtship display by some of the male Ruffs that visit the reserves each spring.

The Washes support the largest British breeding colonies of Black-tailed Godwits, as well as important numbers of Lapwings, Redshank, Snipe and Little Ringed Plovers. Ducks breeding include Tufted Duck, Shelduck, Gadwall and Garganey. There is a good range of smaller birds, too, such as Yellow Wagtails, Reed Buntings, and scarce Tree Sparrows.

consist of a mosaic of grazed or harvested 'lawns', tussocks of grass or sedge, and small pools, providing exactly the right conditions for ducks and waders.

Careful control of other aspects of this special habitat is also essential for wildlife to flourish, including the planting of beds of Osier Willows and pollarding them to ensure a constant crop of new stems that provide nesting cover for ducks and small birds. Reserve staff work with wildfowlers and anglers to minimise disturbance to wildlife, while hides provide birdwatchers with excellent viewpoints.

Abundant Birdlife

Winter brings the greatest number of wildfowl, with up to 900 Mute Swans and the largest wintering concentration of Whooper Swans in England: up to 1,200 arrive each year from their breeding grounds in Iceland. Even greater numbers of Bewick's Swans winter here after journeying from

Other Wildlife

Over 400 species of plants have been recorded, including almost half of all the native British aquatic plants, and species that have become scarce nationally. In the open water these include the rare Fringed Water Lily, as well as Arrowhead and different species of pondweeds and hornworts. Fringing the ditches are masses of Yellow Flag, contrasting with Water Forget-me-not, Common Comfrey and Purple Loosestrife.

The 21 species of dragonflies and damselflies that have been recorded include several scarce or local species, such as the Scarce Chaser and Red-eyed Damselfly. Butterflies abound, including typical grassland species such as Gatekeeper and Common Blue. The waters are home to an impressive range of aquatic invertebrates, including rarities such as the Compressed River Mussel, while fishes include many Eels, Bream, Perch, the rare Spined Loach, and Pike and Rudd, which both grow to a great size.

Water Voles have one of their main British strongholds here. There are also Water Shrews and tiny Harvest Mice (the British Isles' smallest rodent), which are primarily nocturnal. Otters have been reintroduced recently and are seen regularly.

Right: *An unforgettable sight – male Ruffs, each with an individual pattern of gaudy ear-tufts and the ruff that gives the species its name, tussle and joust for dominance at their communal display ground, or 'lek'.*

BRECKLAND

Grassy Heaths and Tall Dark Pines

That part of East Anglia known as Breckland, or The Brecks, occupies about 780 square kilometres (330 square miles) of land, mostly in Norfolk. It is an area of light, dry, sandy and chalky soils, containing many flints, with low rainfall, hot dry summers and cold winters – a climate similar to that of the dry steppes and heathlands of the European continent.

History

Neolithic peoples began to clear the forest here, using flint axes and fire (slash-and-burn), since the soil proved suitable for crop-growing and livestock. Just north of the little town of Brandon is the famous archaeological site of Grimes Graves, not an ancient burial site but the remains of 4,500-year old Neolithic flint mines.

The destruction of the forest continued apace, and as early as Roman times, and especially during the Anglo-Saxon period (5th–10th century AD), huge numbers of sheep grazed the treeless heathlands. Thetford, the central settlement of Breckland, today a small town, was then one of the greatest cities in England, and at times the capital. The Breckland countryside, however, was only very sparsely populated, most of its inhabitants having been driven off the land to make way for sheep.

However, the great sheep boom eventually destroyed the fragile grasslands. With the trees long gone, there was nothing to stop the winds blowing

Top right: *Breckland is one of the few sites where Maiden Pink grows in Britain.*

the thin layer of sandy topsoil away. Sandstorms buried much of the land and many settlements, and large systems of dunes developed. Rabbits were encouraged to breed there and were regularly harvested for their meat by 'warreners'.

By the beginning of the 20th century Breckland was far from thriving, and the land was given over to the cult of pheasant shooting, then at its height.

Major Changes

Shelter belts of conifers were planted during the 19th century to stabilize the soil. Large-scale afforestation began not long after the formation of the Forestry Commission in 1919 to produce home-grown timber after the First World War. From 1922, huge numbers of native Scots Pines and introduced Corsican Pines were planted. The largest plantation, Thetford Forest, is one of the biggest in Britain, covering over 200 square kilometres (77 square miles) today.

In 1954–5, myxomatosis was introduced to Britain to control the huge population of rabbits, a major agricultural pest. Within a few years the effects of their massive decline became apparent in Breckland: much of the heathland was reverting to scrub, and the specialized low-growing wildflowers were threatened. This in turn affected the local wildlife.

The advent of modern farming techniques – very effective fertilizers, machinery, improved irrigation and pesticides – gradually enabled more of the land to be cultivated for crops. Today, Breckland is a mosaic of great arable fields, sand and gravel quarries,

Location: Mostly in Norfolk, between Swaffham (north), Bury St Edmunds (south), East Harling (east) and Lakenheath (west), centred on Thetford.

Climate: Continental-type, with low rainfall, hot dry summers and cold winters.

When to Go: Spring/summer best for breeding birds (Stone Curlews April–August, Nightjars May–early September), wildflowers, reptiles, butterflies and other insects.

Access: By road, via A11, A134, A1088 or A1066 to Thetford for local forest sites. then via A11 and A1075 to East Wretham Heath Norfolk Wildlife Trust reserve; Weeting Heath NNR just north west of Brandon on a minor road off A1065; Grimes Graves via local road between A1065 and A134; Cavenham Heath NNR via A11 and A1101, then via track from just west off Icklingham; Anglo Saxon Village Reconstruction at West Stow, via minor roads off A1101. By rail to Thetford (main line) or Brandon (local service) then local buses.

Permits: Free access to northern part of Cavenham Heath NNR only April–July, otherwise by permit from English Nature.

Equipment: No special equipment required.

Facilities: Most accommodation in Thetford; camp/caravan sites elsewhere. Forest Enterprise and other nature trails; hides at Weeting Heath.

Watching Wildlife: Birdlife, including Stone Curlews and Nightjars, and very elusive Golden Pheasants and Goshawks; also deer, good reptile fauna, special insects and wildflowers.

Visitor Activities: Birdwatching, botany, entomology and general natural history, walking, cycling, archaeology.

Strange Waders

Breckland's speciality is the Stone Curlew, a large wader with an often curiously hunchbacked stance. Its long yellow legs with bulging 'knee' joints (actually ankles) give it its old name 'thick-knee'; it is also known locally as the Norfolk Plover, and is active mainly at dusk. The first birds arrive in March, and by October they have formed flocks ready to fly back to winter in southern Europe and North Africa.

The Norfolk Wildlife Trust reserve at Weeting Heath is the best place to get excellent views of Stone Curlews resting during the day. About half of Britain's breeding population nests in Breckland, many on large stony ploughed fields, with increasing success, thanks to the co-operation of sympathetic farmers.

Oases of Reserves

East Wretham NNR has diverse habitats including wildflowers suited to acid heath, lime-loving species where the sand lies thinly over chalk, and old broadleaved woodlands and several meres. A special feature of Breckland, these are seasonal lakes in which the water level rises or falls in relation to the water table. Tench abound, and there are breeding Little Grebes, Moorhens, Coots and various ducks, including Gadwall. Cavenham Heath NNR is one

golf courses, military bases, and built-up areas – and patches of undeveloped land. The birds and animals typical of the area now mainly survive in nature reserves and in the 70 square kilometres (27 square miles) of the Army's Stanford training grounds, from which the public are excluded. Two special Breckland birds, the spectacular Great Bustard and Red-backed Shrike, have disappeared completely, the former in 1832, the latter in 1988.

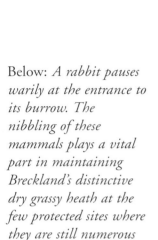

of the finest remaining acid heaths, with a great range of plants, including damp-loving species along the River Lark. Plants thrive that are extremely scarce elsewhere in Britain, such as Breckland Thyme. Insects include dung beetles such as the Trident Beetle, which specializes in burying rabbit-droppings as food for its larvae, and butterflies.

Forest Wildlife

Although the tall dark pines of Thetford Forest can seem relatively devoid of wildlife, the Forestry Commission balances its commercial aims with an impressive conservation policy. Populations of Nightjars and, most dramatically, those of Wood-larks (with one of the most beautiful songs of any British bird), have shown encouraging increases.

The 5.6-kilometre (3½-mile) long Thetford Forest Bird Trail is an excellent way of seeing the range of birdlife in the different areas of clear felling, young trees and more mature forest. There are many rare insects, Red Squirrels are being reintroduced, and Red, Roe and Fallow Deer have lived in the forest since it was established. Another deer, the little Munt-jac, has been introduced more recently. Mayday Farm Forest Trail is one of the best sites for seeing Goshawks, which breed in small numbers.

Above: *The Adder, Britain's only venomous snake, is common in the warm, dry Breckland landscape. It varies considerably in background colour, from pale individuals like this to almost black ones, but a dark zigzag line down the back and V mark on the back of the head usually identify it. Females are mainly duller and thicker.*

MINSMERE/EAST SUFFOLK HEATHS

A Haven for Wildlife

Location: On the Suffolk coast; Minsmere is 39 km (24 miles) north of Ipswich and south of Southwold. East Suffolk Heaths lie immediately to the north.

Climate: Relatively dry; generally warm, sunny summers and cold winters; can be windy.

When to Go: Any time of year for birds, spring/summer for wildflowers and most butterflies, other insects and reptiles.

Access: By road, via A12 from London and Ipswich, then B1125 or B1122 to Minsmere, Dunwich Heath via minor road Westleton–Dunwich, Walberswick via B1387, then public footpaths between Walberswick and Blythburgh. By rail to Darsham (6.5 km/4 miles from Minsmere) on local Ipswich–Lowestoft line. Local buses few and infrequent (nearest stop is Theberton, 5 km (3 miles) away). Suffolk Coastal Path Lowestoft–Felixstowe.

Permits: None necessary.

Equipment: No special equipment required.

Facilities: Varied accommodation: hotels, B&Bs, self-catering cottages and camp/caravan sites in locality, including villages of Eastbridge, Westleton, Middleton, Yoxford, Walberswick and Blythburgh, and small towns of Saxmundham, Aldeburgh and Southwold. Nature trails, guided walks; at Minsmere, visitor centre, shop, café, 8 hides, programme of events for all ages.

Watching Wildlife: Superb birdlife: famous Avocets at Minsmere; rich insect fauna, many butterflies and dragonflies; special wildflowers and a wide range of reptiles.

Visitor Activities: Birdwatching, entomology, botany and general natural history, walking, cycling.

The most famous nature reserve in Britain, the 800-hectare (2,000-acre) Minsmere RSPB reserve, on the Suffolk coast, is a paradise for naturalists and one of the best places to see a variety of birds and other wildlife. It is also internationally recognized as an example of how hard work and patience can create a premier reserve.

Minsmere has a whole range of different lowland habitats: beach, sand dunes, an artificial coastal lagoon with brackish water and mud, a large reedbed, a small area of flower-rich pasture, woodland and heathland, ensuring a wide range of wildlife. Over 300 species of birds have been recorded, of which 200 are seen annually. More than 100 of these breed each year, more than in any other reserve or comparable area in the British Isles. Other wildlife include over 460 species of moths, 33 species of butterflies and 650 species of plants.

Top left: *Tiny Muntjac Deer, introduced to Britain from China in about 1900.*

Opposite, top: *Dunwich Heath in August.*

Opposite, bottom left: *One of Minsmere's star birds is the Marsh Harrier: this is a female.*

Opposite, bottom centre: *Nature trail sign posting.*

Opposite, bottom right: *Minsmere's mammals include the appealing little Wood Mouse.*

Rich Birdlife

Minsmere is almost unparalleled in Britain in its variety of breeding, migrating and wintering birds. Spring is a delightful time, when the woodland birds can be seen more easily before the foliage has become dense. Each morning is greeted by a wonderful dawn chorus from both residents – for example Song Thrushes, Robins and Chaffinches – and migrants such as Blackcaps, Garden Warblers, Willow Warblers, Chiffchaffs and Redstarts. Nightingales favour coppiced areas of woodland with bramble thickets, from where the males pour out their glorious song by day and night.

A visit to the reedbeds is worthwhile at any time of year. This is one of the best places in Britain to see the elusive Bittern, while Kingfishers often fish from perches near the hides, Marsh Harriers sail majestically past, and little flocks of Bearded Tits whirr low over the reeds. Now and then a rarity such as a Spoonbill causes extra excitement among the human occupants of the hides.

The Return of the Avocet

It is fitting that the symbol of the RSPB is the Avocet, as the society was instrumental in bringing this graceful black-and-white wader with its curiously upcurved bill back to breed in Britain. After an absence of more than 150 years 28 birds returned in 1947 to nest at Minsmere, as well as at Havergate Island further down the coast. The habitat was created after coastal marshland at Minsmere Level

Above: *The contrast-ingly coloured flowers of gorses and heathers in close-up at Dunwich Heath.*

that had been reclaimed during the 18th century was deliberately flooded by opening the sea sluices during the Second World War as a defence against expected German invasion. The RSPB leased this promising site and began to create a reserve.

One of the most important habitats is the artificial 'Scrape' (imitated at many other reserves), a mosaic of shallow open water, wet mud and small bare or vegetated shingle islands, produced using a combination of heavy earth-moving machinery and back-breaking excavation by hand. Maintaining optimum conditions for the many waders, including the Avocets, that feed on the mud necessitates careful control of the level and salinity of the water by means of sluices. Waders are present at every season, but spring and autumn passage is the most exciting time of year, when a great variety of species – almost 50 have been recorded over the years – stop to rest and refuel here on their long migration to and from their Arctic breeding grounds.

Anther important management task on the Scrape's artificial islands is regular trimming of the vegetation (both by hand and by a herd of Konik Polish Ponies) to maintain a suitable habitat for the Avocets and other waders and the Common Terns that nest on them. Scarce fast-flying Little Terns breed too, protected from human disturbance in a cordoned-off area of the sand and shingle beach.

The East Suffolk Heaths

These are remnants of the sheep-grazed Sandlings that once formed an almost unbroken strip of heathland along the east Suffolk coast, extending for some 40 kilometres (25 miles) northwards from near Ipswich as far as Blythburgh. Today only a few scattered areas remain untouched, the rest having

been reclaimed for agriculture, forestry, sand or gravel quarrying, airfields, golf courses, houses and a variety of other developments.

These precious remnants are protected within four main nature reserves, two of which form the northern border with Minsmere's heathland. West-leton Heath NNR is a 47-hectare (117-acre) area bordering Dunwich Heath SSSI, whose 86.5 hectares (214 acres) are owned by the National Trust. In addition to the reserves, the Suffolk coast and heaths are an AONB.

On these splendid heaths, Common Heather grows together with Bell Heather, while pink-and-purple Cross-leaved Heath forms a glorious, sweet-smelling carpet in damper areas in summer. The heathers contrast with the rich yellow flowers of Common, Western and Dwarf Gorse. Parasitic Common Dodder twines its thin reddish stems around both heathers and gorse, extracting nutrients from them via suckers.

Breeding birds of the Suffolk Sandlings include Woodlarks and Tree Pipits, as well as Nightjars with their strange, mechanical, churring song around dusk and into the night, when the lights of Glow-worms twinkle like stars fallen to earth. In winter you may see a Great Grey Shrike perched atop a gorse bush or a Rough-legged Buzzard hovering on broad wings. More regularly visiting birds of prey are Hen Harriers and Merlins.

There are panoramic views of Minsmere's woods and marshes from the low, sandy Minsmere Cliffs that border the seaward side of Dunwich Heath. On the long straight shingle beach, characteristic plants include the attractive Yellow Horned-poppy and purple-and-blue-flowered Sea Pea.

Dunwich itself – or what little remains of it – is worth a visit. In medieval times it was a bustling city, the seat of the King of East Anglia and the largest port on the Suffolk coast. Over the centuries the soft cliffs were eroded away by the sea – about 1.6 kilometres (1 mile) of land has vanished over the last 1,000 years – and the great medieval town gradually disappeared beneath the waves: the last of 12 churches toppled into the cold North Sea in 1919. Dunwich is now little more than a single street of Victorian houses, a museum that tells the story of the lost city, a pub, and the remains of Greyfriars monastery, hanging precariously at the cliff edge.

The northernmost of these protected areas is the 605-hectare (1,500-acre) Walberswick NNR, which includes one of the best surviving areas of heathland, as well as mudflats, saltmarsh, woodland and the biggest continuous freshwater reedbed in Britain, which is no more than 55 years old. There is a variety of wetland plants here, including Sea Lavender, Sea Purslane and Sea Aster on the saltmarshes and Wild Celery, Marsh Pennywort and the rare Fen Sow-thistle. Rare Wainscot Moths breed among the reeds.

Above: *Avocet and chick – this graceful wader breeds at Minsmere on the shingle islands of the Scrape.*

Below: *A view across the Scrape – a carefully managed artifically created habitat at Minsmere that attracts many wetland birds.*

THE BROADS NATIONAL PARK

A World of Water

This is one of the most extensive areas of wetlands in Britain, with over 40 shallow, reed-fringed lakes, or broads, many connected to the river systems by dykes. Five major rivers – the Bure, its tributaries the Ant and Thurne, the Yare and the Waveney – wind through flat marshlands before entering the vast tidal basin of Breydon Water, which meets the North Sea at Great Yarmouth.

The Broads can be a beautiful, tranquil area where water and land seem to merge into one, but it is also a very popular holiday destination. With 201 kilometres (125 miles) of safe, lock-free navigable waterways, many visitors choose to see the Broads by hiring boats – including house-boats and historic sailing barges called wherries – and the rivers and broads can become very crowded in summer.

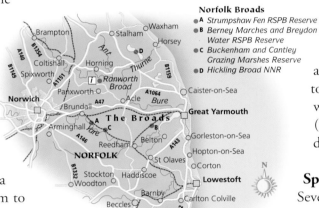

Norfolk Broads
- **A** *Strumpshaw Fen RSPB Reserve*
- **B** *Berney Marches and Breydon Water RSPB Reserve*
- **C** *Buckenham and Cantley Grazing Marshes Reserve*
- **D** *Hickling Broad NNR*

Surprising Origins

This huge area was long thought to be a natural feature, the remains of a great estuary, most of which had become silted up thousands of years ago. But new research published in 1953 showed that the expanses of open water and many of the adjacent fens were caused by the extensive excavation of peat during the Middle Ages for the growing populations of cities such as Norwich. Instead of naturally sloping edges, the watercourses and broads have vertical sides where the peat has been cut out.

Top left: *A striking male Bearded Tit.*

Opposite: *The ancient craft of reed cutting in progress at How Hill in February.*

Rising sea levels, especially in the 14th century, resulted in many of the excavations being abandoned as they filled with water to produce the broads we see today. The bigger broads were created by the flooding of the deeper peat workings, but many of the shallower ones have disappeared as reedbeds have dried out to form fen, then scrub, wet Alder woodland (called 'carr') and finally drier woodland.

Special Birds

Several species of birds are particularly associated with the Broads. The Bittern, a big, extremely wary member of the heron family, thrived in the extensive reedbeds until the early 19th century. Its striped camouflage enabled it to remain invisible, the only evidence of its presence usually being the deep, sonorous booming calls of the males. By the mid-19th century, drainage of wetlands, hunting and cold winters had taken their toll. After becoming effectively extinct by 1868, it returned to nest in the Broads in 1911. By 1954, there were peak populations of 55 males in Broadland, but since then numbers have declined, due mainly to water pollution. Nowadays only one or two pairs breed here, although more visit in winter.

Bearded Tits, too, have suffered, their populations ebbing in response to environmental conditions and especially the effects of hard winters. Today they seem to be declining, despite a series of relatively mild winters.

The story of the Marsh Harrier is a happier one. Previously abundant in its Broadland stronghold, drainage and persecution led to its extinction in Britain by the end of the 19th century. Although it

Above: *The Grass Snake, Britain's biggest snake, is a non-venomous species that favours ditches, slow-moving streams and other wetland habitats, including the Broads. It has two distinctive yellow or white patches on its neck.*

Right: *A Swallowtail Butterfly at Hickling Broad, by the Weaver's Way, a long-distance path that passes through Broadland. This striking insect breeds in the British Isles only in the Broads.*

Far right: *The Otter occurs in Broadland where pollution and riverbank damage have not taken their toll. Shy and mainly nocturnal, it is hard to see: you are more likely to find evidence of its presence in the form of its tarry droppings (or 'spraints'), shiny with the scales of its fish prey.*

returned to the Broads, it remained a rare breeder until the mid-1970s, but today, after a dramatic comeback, about 25 pairs breed here.

Places to Visit

Lying only 4.8 kilometres (3 miles) from the sea, Hickling Broad NNR is the largest of the broads, and is owned and leased by the Norfolk Wildlife Trust. A boardwalk path takes the visitor through extensive reedbeds, where (as throughout the Broads) the famous Norfolk thatch is still cut each year and used for roofing houses. Here there are Reed and Sedge Warblers, Reed Buntings and other birds. Another path leads to a dragonfly pool; a third leads through the grazing marshes, where Redshank and Yellow Wagtails nest. An impressive range of waders, especially in spring and autumn passage periods, can be seen; migrant Black Terns are best spotted in spring, hawking for insects. There is a wide range of other waterbirds, especially in winter, and, in common with other Broadland reserves, a rich flora, including orchids and scarce water plants.

Strumpshaw Fen RSPB Reserve, in the Yare Valley 10 kilometres (6 miles) east of Norwich, is part of the mid-Yare NNR. Its open water, reedbeds, carr woodland and grazing marshes attract a wide range of wetland birds, including Marsh Harriers floating across the reeds where Bearded Tits also breed, Cetti's Warblers in the carrs, and, with luck, a migrant Osprey in spring or autumn.

Mammals include elusive Water Shrews, Water Voles and little, introduced, Chinese Water Deer. Among the highlights are the handsome Swallowtail butterflies, which breed only on a few protected fens and marshes in East Anglia, all in the Broads. The caterpillars feed on the rare Milk Parsley, while the gorgeous adults, Britain's largest resident butterflies, are on the wing from mid-May until early July, with a second brood in August in warmer years. The Norfolk Hawker dragonfly, found only at a few Broadland sites, is dependent on a strange water plant, Water Soldier, that moves up and down in the water-filled ditches.

Buckenham and Cantley grazing marshes by the River Yare near Strumpshaw are the only regular wintering site in Britain for the Taiga Bean Goose. The birds tend to be present from mid-November, and have usually left by early March to migrate to their breeding grounds in northern Sweden.

Overlooking Ranworth Broad, north of the A47 road, 1.6 kilometres (10 miles) north-east of Norwich, the Broadland Conservation Centre is reached via a duckboard trail through typical Broadland environments. The centre features displays on the history and wildlife of the area.

Caring for the Broads

The fragile environment of this very special part of Britain has deteriorated in quality, especially over the last 30 years. The water has become polluted, chiefly from the run-off of nitrates from fertilizers and the build-up of phosphates from inadequately treated sewage. Massive growths of minute algae block the sunlight and prevent the growth of aquatic plants. Toxins from the algae have killed large numbers of fish, and toxins released by bacteria in the mud have wiped out thousands of wildfowl.

A huge increase in the number of powered boats using the Broads has also contributed to the problem by stirring up sediment, eroding the fragile banks, destroying aquatic vegetation, and disturbing wildlife. Many reedbeds have shrunk, with the loss of many of the animals that depend on them.

Conservation bodies are trying to improve the situation. Several broads have been isolated by building embankments, and the mud has been pumped out to remove the dead algae and pollutants.

Above: *Sailing is an extremely popular and attractive way of enjoying the Broads.*

Left: *Hunched in a characteristic stance, a Bittern relies on its striped plumage to camouflage it against the reed stems.*

THE NORTH NORFOLK COAST

Lonely Bird-rich Shores

The coast of north Norfolk is one of the most splendid in Europe, a wild, remote world of great expanses of sand and mud stretching to the horizon under a vast sky. Huge stretches of saltmarsh, among the largest in Britain, dissected by intricate networks of channels, echo to the haunting cries of Curlews and other waders. There are sand dunes, shingle spits and beaches, coastal lagoons, reedbeds and pine plantations, a few small towns and attractive villages, old fishermen's cottages and churches faced with smooth flint pebbles, windmills and welcoming pubs.

For over 32 kilometres (20 miles), much of the land lying along the coast to the west of the resort towns of Cromer and Sheringham, from Cley to Holme, is protected in a chain of nature reserves; this is Britain's prime birdwatching area. It is also a wonderful place for sea anglers, sailors of yachts and other small boats, and all who love wild places.

Its great diversity of habitats and geographical position makes the north Norfolk coast a magnet for migrating birds seeking a landfall to rest and feed before continuing on their way.

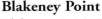

North Norfolk Coast map

Top left: *A view at Blakeney Harbour.*

Opposite, top: *A huge flock of Knots pack tightly together as they gather at their roost.*

Opposite, bottom left: *Sea Lavender.*

Opposite, bottom right: *Scarce migrants seen regularly here include the Bluethroat.*

Cley Marshes

Cley-next-the-Sea, like many of the north Norfolk coast villages, is actually situated some distance inland. Like Blakeney to the west, Cley (pronounced 'Cly') was in medieval times a major port for export of wool from the rich sheep country of north Norfolk. Today it is a great place to escape from it all.

Cley Marshes has been a mecca for birdwatchers for over 80 years. This splendid stretch of shore is a Norfolk Wildlife Trust reserve: indeed, it was the first property to be acquired by what was then the Norfolk Naturalists' Trust, the original such organization in Britain, in 1926. The scrapes – artificially created lagoons – help to make this the best place in Britain for seeing migrant waders, including rare, off-course wanderers. There are breeding Bitterns, Garganeys and Avocets, too, while migrant petrels, shearwaters, Gannets, sea ducks, skuas, gulls and terns pass offshore in autumn.

Blakeney Point

Blakeney Point NNR, purchased by the National Trust in 1912, lies at the end of a long, constantly changing shingle spit. It can be reached by boat from Blakeney Quay or Morston Quay but the exhausting 5-kilometre (3-mile) walk from Cley along the shingle is often rewarded in spring and autumn by plenty of interesting birds.

On a map, the Point, at the end of the arm of the shingle ridge, resembles an oversized hand with its index finger pointing down at the coast. At its end is a large breeding colony of terns, mostly Sandwich

Opposite, top: *Razor shells washed up on a north Norfolk beach after a storm in January.*

Opposite, centre: *One of the loveliest plants of the shingle is the Yellow Horned Poppy, seen here at Blakeney Point.*

Opposite, bottom: *A pair of Grey Seals relax in The Wash.*

Right: *The Barn Owl finds one of its strongholds in the north Norfolk coastal marshes.*

Below: *Titchwell RSPB reserve. As well as being Britain's premier birding area, the north Norfolk coast is a Heritage Coast.*

Terns, but also Common and scarce Little Terns and sometimes a few Arctic Terns, at the southern limit of their breeding range. There are major 'falls' of migrants, especially in spring and, to a lesser extent, in autumn. As well as the usual species these include rare birds such as Hoopoes, Barred Warblers, Red-breasted Flycatchers, Bluethroats and Firecrests, all of which are seen each year.

Common Seals breed off the Point and boat trips to see them (and a few Grey Seals) are run from Blakeney Quay in summer. These are the outliers of the great breeding populations on the sandbanks in the Wash.

During the late 19th century, the large area of dunes at Holkham Gap were stabilized with Corsican Pines, and today this beautiful woodland runs down to the shore. This is a popular site for birdwatchers in late summer and autumn, when there are large number of migrants from across the North Sea. On either side of these woods the largest coastal NNR in England extends for 19 kilometres (12 miles) from Overy Staithe to Blakeney, covering an area of almost 4,000 hectares (10,000 acres).

At Brancaster, over 6.4 km (4 miles) of saltmarsh, mud and sand flats and tall dunes are owned by the National Trust and designated as an SSSI. Here, as elsewhere along this coast, the fleshy bright green young stems of Glasswort plants, known locally as samphire, are gathered from the saltmarshes and sold to be eaten as a traditional delicacy, one seen increasingly on the menus of London restaurants.

Scolt Head Island NNR, safely accessible only by boat, is a marvellously wild place. It has a fine succession of saltmarsh and dune plants, and is filled with the harsh screams of nesting terns in spring and summer, as well as attracting huge numbers of migrant passerines.

The Wash Coast

At its western end, the Norfolk coast turns abruptly south to border The Wash, a huge bay 24 kilometres (15 miles) long and 40 kilometres (25 miles) wide, between Norfolk and Lincolnshire. Four major rivers – the Nene, Great Ouse, Welland and Witham – drain into this vast estuary. Although much land has been reclaimed for agriculture, there are still large areas of saltmarsh, and at low tides vast sands and mudflats.

The Wash is of international importance for its populations of wintering waders. Huge numbers of

Knots, Redshank, Dunlin and other species probe the glistening mud for the rich concentrations of buried invertebrate prey, or take to the air, their flocks forming intricate shifting patterns like drifting smoke as they wheel and turn in perfect unison. Ducks of many species, including up to about 23,000 Shelduck, as well as 9,000 Pink-footed Geese and 24,000 of the dark-bellied race of the Brent Goose, also visit the area. The Wash is also the most important single site for Common Seals in the British Isles, with up to 7,000 of these mammals.

Titchwell (379 hectares/936 acres) has overtaken Minsmere to become the RSPB's most visited reserve. Its 80 breeding species include Marsh Harriers, Bitterns, Avocets, Little Terns, Bearded Tits and Reed Buntings. This is an excellent spot for Little Egrets and Spoonbills, and a lone male Black-winged Stilt has spent eight years at the reserve.

Hunstanton is the only resort town on the East Anglian coast to face westwards, and is also distinguished by its candy-striped cliffs, with red chalk sandwiched between white chalk and a brown sandstone known as carr stone. They provide a good site for Fulmars to nest.

One of the world's greatest wildlife spectacles takes place twice a day at Snettisham RSPB reserve. As the tide advances over the vast mudflats of The Wash, thousands upon thousands of waders stop feeding and fly to their roosts off the beach.

NORTHERN ENGLAND

IN THIS BOOK, THE LARGE AREA OF LAND MAKING UP NORTHERN ENGLAND – 49,812 square kilometres (19,234 square miles) in total – is considered to extend from a line joining The Wash estuary in the east and the Dee estuary in the west, north to the Scottish border. Although there are areas of flat terrain – such as the Vale of Pickering and Vale of York – much of the 'North Country' is a rugged upland landscape, markedly different in character from the gentler, milder southern regions of England.

The Pennine chain of hills, the 'backbone' of northern England, extends some 240

kilometres (150 miles) north from the Peak District in the south of the region via the Yorkshire Dales to the Cheviot Hills and Scottish borderlands. Much of it can be walked by following the Pennine Way, Britain's first long-distance footpath.

There are five National Parks: the Peak District, first in England and Wales and containing two very different landscapes, the sombre Dark Peak and the softer White Peak; the largest, the Lake District, with its world-famous scenery and England's highest mountains; the Yorkshire Dales, where valley farmland contrasts with wild fellsides, creating a landscape of great beauty; the North York Moors, with its glorious heather moorland and spectacular coast; and the most remote, Northumberland. The great variety of habitats includes mountain and moorland, lakes and rivers, forests, limestone pavements and major cave systems, supporting upland plants and wildlife at their southernmost limits.

The coasts hold some of the least visited and most beautiful stretches of shoreline in all England, with dune systems, long sandy beaches, sea cliffs and rocky islands, home to a myriad of animals and plants. Morecambe Bay attracts vast numbers of waders in winter, while the Farne Islands off Northumberland are renowned for their seabird colonies.

Opposite, left: *The Natterjack Toad, Britain's rarest native amphibian, has its stronghold on the coasts of north-west Britain.*

Below: *Ullswater, the Lake District's second largest lake at over 13 km (8 miles) long, is one of the most beautiful and unspoilt. Paths wind along its shoreline, giving stunning views and passing through a variety of habitats.*

THE PEAK DISTRICT NATIONAL PARK

Two Worlds in One Park

Location: In the centre of England, mainly in Derbyshire.

Climate: The White Peak has a windier, cloudier, frostier climate than the surrounding lowlands; summers can be warm and sunny; the Dark Peak is more changeable, with some harsh weather.

When to Go: All year for walking (essential to be well prepared on high ground), spring and summer for flowers, breeding birds and butterflies; autumn for heather in bloom.

Access: By road, turn west from M1 at exit 28/29 for south of Park, exit 31 for centre, or exit 36 for north. A515 Ashbourne–Buxton and A6 Matlock–Manchester cross the Park. By rail, local trains from Manchester to Glossop in the north or Buxton in the south, or via the Hope Valley line (5 stations in the Park); buses serve most areas. The 435-km (270-mile) Pennine Way long-distance footpath begins at Kinder Scout.

Permits: None required.

Equipment: Fleece and water-proofs can be required all year.

Facilities: Largest range of accommodation in Buxton and Castleton; plenty also in Ashbourne, Matlock, Glossop and Buxton, on the Park's fringes; 16 youth hostels and 9 camping barns; 15 NP information centres.

Watching Wildlife: White Peak famous for limestone-loving wildflowers and river wildlife; Dark Peak has breeding grouse, waders, scarce birds of prey and interesting birdlife.

Visitor Activities: Walking, climbing, caving, cycling, horse riding, fishing, gliding, hang gliding, birdwatching, botany, general natural history.

Established in 1951, the 1,438-square-kilometre (555-square-mile) Peak District National Park was Britain's first, providing much-needed 'lungs' for the huge urban area surrounding it. With half the total population of England living within 96 kilometres (60 miles) it's no surprise that some claim this to be the second-most-visited National Park in the world, after Japan's Mount Fuji.

One of the main reasons for the Park's creation was the great demand from the people of the industrial northern cities for access to the moors, protected by their wealthy owners for grouse shooting. This culminated in the 'Battle of Kinder Scout' in April 1932, when a mass trespass by ramblers resulted not only in the arrests of some of the leaders, but also in the recognition of a need for better access and for the protection of the precious Peak landscapes from development.

Today, many of the best areas for scenery and wildlife are national and local nature reserves, SSSIs, SACs and ESAs. Despite this, there are still threats from limestone quarrying and the sheer numbers of tourists.

The name of this region derives from the Old English *peac*, meaning hill, before the word was used to define a pointed summit. Another twist of language has led to the word 'low'

Top left: Lathkill, in the White Peak, is among the last places in Britain to see wild Jacob's Ladder.

Opposite: The Salt Cellar Tor, Derwent Edge, one of many dramatic rocky outcrops of the Dark Peak.

(from the Old English word *hlaw*, meaning hill or burial mound) being frequently used to mark a high point – there is even a 'High Low' on the hill above Hope valley!

As you enter the Peak District from the gentle, fertile land to the south you notice a dramatic change in the scenery. The rugged landscapes of the Peak form the first 64 kilometres (40 miles) of the Pennines, the great upland chain that forms England's backbone, extending 240 kilometres (150 miles) north to the Scottish border. Fields of crops bordered with hedges give way to rough hill pasture, divided by a network of drystone walls, craftsman-built from the local limestone, and lonely hills with moors and bogs. The climate is distinctly cooler and wetter.

The Peak District divides naturally into two contrasting areas, named from the very different types of rock and landscapes they contain.

The White Peak

In the south and centre is the gentler, prettier White Peak, a much-eroded plateau of pale limestone. This is a land of deep dales, where fast-flowing streams run through towering, steep-sided valleys. Many are too narrow for roads, and are ideal for the walker who wants to get away from it all. Several former railway lines, such as the Monsal Trail, have been converted to make splendid tracks for ramblers, cyclists and horse riders.

Along with tourism, farming is one of the major occupations, and the rolling fields are grazed by cattle and sheep. Much of the land is 'improved' for growing short-term grass leys, and many of the old flower-rich meadows have been lost. However,

protected areas do remain, glorious in spring and summer with abundant wildflowers and butterflies.

The Dark Peak

The starkly dramatic Dark Peak encircles the White Peak like a great inverted horseshoe. The underlying rock is millstone grit, and the landscape consists of great tracts of lonely, dark moorland covered by blanket bog. This is some of the wildest country in England, especially in the high northern moors around Bleaklow, Black Hill and Kinder Scout, at 636 metres (2,087 feet) the highest point in the Peak District.

These forbidding places have been created by centuries of grazing and burning by man. Countless furrows of dark-chocolate-brown banks of peat

('hags') stretch for mile after mile, broken up by deep natural drainage channels containing dark, acid water ('groughs'). There are few signs of life apart from clumps of cotton grasses, their fluffy white heads waving in the wind, and the thin cheepings of Meadow Pipits.

The best time for seeing the special birds here is in spring and early summer. Red Grouse were the main reason for the establishment of areas of heather on the drier moors, and grouse shooting continues today at a reduced level, since the birds' breeding success suffers increasingly from the effects of parasitic worms.

A select group of waders breed here. Golden Plovers, 'the watchmen of the moors', utter their plaintive piping alarm calls. Curlew pour out their glorious bubbling courtship songs, while you may also hear the rich purring trills of little Dunlin and the strange bleating, or 'drumming', of Snipe, resulting from wind rushing over the male's stiff outer tail feathers. Other nesting birds include Twite, the upland cousin of the Linnet – now very scarce – and Ring Ouzels, which like to nest by the steep-sided, narrow ravines, known as 'cloughs'.

This is also a good place for Kestrels, dashing little Merlins and powerful Peregrines, as well as Hen Harriers and Short-eared Owls.

The Peak's 'Lake District'

To supply water to the huge populations nearby, the Upper Derwent valley has been dammed in many places to form reservoirs; there are more than 50 in the Park. The deep, acid waters support relatively few birds, but Red-breasted Mergansers and Common Sandpipers can be seen there. Great belts of conifers around many of these artificial lakes contain interesting birds such as Goldcrests, the smallest birds in Europe, Coal Tits, Siskins and Crossbills. The conifer forests around the largest reservoir, Ladybower, are good places for seeing the Goshawk, the bigger cousin of the Sparrowhawk, which is much rarer in Britain. Ideally, look on fine windless days in March and April when pairs perform display flights.

Recreation

The varied landscapes have always been extremely popular with walkers and cyclists. Only some 24 kilometres (15 miles) from the great city of Manchester, the eastern edge of the Black Peak forms impressive gritstone cliffs that provide tough challenges for rock-climbers: the sport of modern rock-climbing was born here.

This is also an important area for caving. The porous limestone rock has been carved away by acid rainwater over millions of years to form spectacular caves, especially in the Hope Valley around the fine medieval town of Castleton, where the limestone meets the millstone grit and shales of the Dark Peak. Many of them were discovered by lead miners in the 18th and 19th centuries. Most are for experienced cavers only, but there are a number of show caverns. The mouth of Peak Cavern is so big that it once sheltered a rope factory and a small village, while Blue John and Treak Cliff Caverns are the world's only source of Blue John, the sparkling semi-precious fluorspar stone.

In the most famous dale, Dovedale, dramatic pinnacles of rock tower above a sparkling river bordered by lovely Ash woods, carpeted in spring with wildflowers. This is one of England's most popular tourist sites and is best avoided at the height of summer.

Angling is an important activity, and the Park contains some of England's finest trout rivers, with abundant wildlife, including Otters, Kingfishers, Dippers, Grey Wagtails, dragonflies, and native White-clawed Crayfish as well as Brown Trout and various other species of fish.

Below: *Well-known landmarks in the western Dark Peak are these broken, folded faces of millstone grit sandstone, known as the Roaches and Hen Cloud.*

MORECAMBE BAY & LEIGHTON MOSS

Vast Sandbanks and Waving Reeds

Location: England's north-west coast, bounded by Lancashire and Cumbria; Leighton Moss is a reclaimed inlet of the bay.

Climate: Spring–autumn warm and sunny, winters generally mild; rainfall relatively frequent; violent storms possible, especially in autumn.

When to Go: Spring/autumn for migrant seabirds/waders/wildfowl; huge numbers of winter-waders/wildfowl; spring/summer for breeding birds, wildflowers and insects at Leighton Moss.

Access: By road, M6 or A6; local roads to coast; Leighton Moss RSPB reserve signposted from A6 north of M6 exit 35a. By rail, main line to Lancaster; local trains to Morecambe and Carnforth for southern end of bay, Silverdale for central part near Leighton Moss, and stations to Barrow-in-Furness for northern end. Good local bus system.

Permits: Required for South Walney reserve (from Warden).

Equipment: Waterproofs are advisable.

Facilities: Hotels/B&Bs in nearby towns; self-catering accommodation, camp/caravan sites and youth hostels. Leighton Moss RSPB reserve has visitor centre/nature trails/hides; More-cambe Bay RSPB reserve has nature trails/hides. Bird ringing station/ observatory on Walney Island, also Cumbria Wildlife Trust South Walney reserve.

Watching Wildlife: Great variety at Leighton Moss; Heysham excellent for spring/autumn bird migrants, and Leach's Petrels September–October.

Visitor Activities: Birdwatching, marine biology, botany, entomology, natural history, walking, fishing.

The name Morecambe was derived from the Celtic name *Mori Cambo* ('Great Bay') for the Lune estuary, one of the five rivers draining into this huge bay, covering over 500 square kilometres (190 square miles). Low tide reveals vast expanses of golden sands and mud, fringed with saltmarsh, concealing a teeming population of molluscs, worms, crustaceans and other invertebrates (up to 50,000 individuals per square metre). This is the single most important site for wintering waders in Britain, and one of the most valuable coastal sites in the whole of Europe, with up to quarter of a million waders and wildfowl including Oystercatchers, Knots, Dunlin, Curlews, Bar-tailed Godwits, dark-bellied Brent Geese, Pink-footed Geese, Wigeon, Pintail and Shelduck. The views inland to the mountains of the Lake District are spectacular.

Venturing out onto the sand and mudflats is not recommended without an experienced guide, as the incoming tide races in with astonishing speed and little warning, and there are dangerous quicksands. Headstones in local cemeteries record the deaths of those who have fallen victim to the rushing water. Regular crossings of the sands are

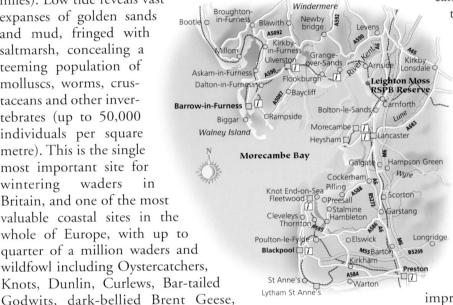

Top left: *The Grasshopper Warbler has declined nationally but still breeds regularly at Leighton Moss RSPB Reserve.*

Opposite, top: *Walney Island at low tide.*

Opposite, bottom: *A view down one of the channels through a reedbed in Leighton Moss RSPB Reserve.*

conducted from Arnside in spring and summer by the official 'Queen's Guide to the Sands'.

Finding the Birds

Looking for birds in Morecambe Bay can be daunting, and it is best to concentrate on a few areas that hold the greatest numbers and variety. The movements of waders depend on the tides: when out, with the sea up to 11.3 kilometres (7 miles) from the coast, the birds are distant, but as the water returns they are driven inshore and forced onto their roosts, where they can be seen at closer range.

The mouth of the Leven estuary and the large area of saltmarsh at Flookburgh Marshes have impressive roosts of waders and wildfowl, which attract hunting birds of prey.

The 19.3-kilometre (12-mile) long, narrow curve of Walney Island consists mainly of sand dunes and grassland. A good site for winter visitors, it is also worth visiting in summer. At its southern tip is a Cumbria Wildlife Trust reserve, with huge breeding colonies – among the biggest in Europe – of Lesser Black-backed and Herring Gulls. South Walney also has breeding Eider Ducks, as well as Sandwich, Common, Arctic and Little Terns.

On either side of the River Keer, saltmarsh at Carnforth Marsh and Hest Bank form a major roost area for waders, gulls and wildfowl, protected as the RSPB's Morecambe Bay reserve. Further up the Keer valley, flooded gravel pits attract Smew and other scarce ducks, Black Terns and Little and Mediterranean Gulls. Other good areas lie along the Kent estuary at the northern corner of the bay, and the Lune estuary towards its southern end.

The small town of Fleetwood, at the southernmost edge, is a good place for viewing a variety of waders and sea-ducks in winter, while autumn's north-westerly gales can bring migrating skuas, gulls, terns and Leach's Petrels close inshore. The best viewpoint is from the promenade at Rossall Point on the town's western edge.

Leighton Moss

This 161-hectare (398-acre) RSPB reserve nestles in a small, wooded, limestone valley, formerly an arm of Morecambe Bay. Its main habitats are extensive reedbeds surrounding shallow freshwater meres, forming one of the largest areas of continuous reeds in the whole of Britain.

This is a major stronghold for Britain's very small breeding population of Bitterns. They are easier to see in May, when looking for food for young, and during winter when the pools freeze and they are forced out into the open to feed. This is also the best time for watching the equally secretive Water Rails. There is also a thriving colony of Bearded Tits, as well as Reed and Sedge Warblers. Skulking Grasshopper Warblers, betrayed by their strange song (like the sound of a fishing reel being wound) favour the patches of willow scrub.

Winter brings many wildfowl, including Mallard and Teal, and smaller numbers of Wigeon, Pintail and Goldeneye, while skeins of Pink-footed and Greylag Geese sometimes pass overhead. From spring, there is also a good range of ducks breeding on the small islands in the meres, including Mallard, Teal, Shoveler, Tufted Duck and Pochard, and Garganey stop over in small numbers on migration. The islets are also used by nesting Moorhens, Coots and colonies of Black-headed Gulls. This is one of the best places in England for Otters, which are regularly seen, especially from the Lower Hide.

The lower flanks of the hills rising from the valley are clothed with Hawthorn, Blackthorn and Ash scrub, giving way higher up to typical limestone woods of Ash, Oak, Birch and Yew. There are Red and Roe Deer here, which venture into the reedbeds to graze on plants. Birdlife includes all three species of British woodpeckers, Robins, Wrens, tits and elusive Hawfinches all year round, and Blackcaps, Garden Warblers, Chiffchaffs and Willow Warblers in summer.

The woodlands and their margins are good places for limestone-loving wildflowers, and the edges are excellent for butterfly watching in July and August. One of Britain's scarcest species, the High Brown Fritillary, flits swiftly above the grassy slopes; Purple Hairstreaks are harder to see, keeping mainly to the crowns of the Ash and Oak trees.

In autumn and winter there are spectacular massed flights of Starlings, involving up to 20,000 birds in synchronized aerobatic displays over the reedbeds at dusk before roosting in them for the night.

YORKSHIRE DALES NATIONAL PARK

Traditional Farming and Nature in Harmony

Britain's third-largest National Park, the Yorkshire Dales, was designated in 1954, covering 1,769 square kilometres (683 square miles). Sandwiched between the Lake District to the west and the North York Moors in the east, almost all of it lies in Yorkshire, although in the north west it includes the Howgill Fells, in Cumbria.

Straddling the great Pennine upland chain, the area offers two contrasting worlds: the long, gauntly beautiful parallel ridges of hills (or 'fells'), covered with mountain grasses or heather, above the lovely 'dales' (long, deep valleys), with sparkling rivers, soft green pastures and meadowland.

Each of the 50 or so dales is different – some remote, narrow and bordered by craggy heights, others broader, lusher and thronged with tourists – but all have that highly characteristic mix of landscape features that draws visitors back again and again. These include stone buildings in the picturesque, neat villages and scattered farms, countless drystone walls crisscrossing the valleys and lower fellsides, and old barns that pepper the little fields. In many areas, especially on the higher plateaux, the underlying rock and local architecture is dark millstone grit, while elsewhere it is softer off-white Carboniferous limestone.

Over 50 per cent of the area is open moorland, 40 per cent farmland, and under 3 per cent woodland. Arguably, no other part of the British landscape is so intimately tied up with human

Top right: A typical Yorkshire Dales hay meadow, including buttercups and Bloody Cranes-bill.

stewardship of the land. Even on the high tops, human presence is reflected by the network of paths and green lanes, once used by sheep drovers and packhorsemen, that now provide wonderful walking opportunities.

Changing History

Farming has created the Dales we see today. Prehistoric peoples cleared most of the woodland; in the 9th and 10th centuries the Norse folk colonized and farmed the area, their influence remaining in many place names: dale is from *dalr*, and fell from *fjall*; 'foss' denotes a waterfall, and many village names end in '-thwaite', meaning a settlement.

This has been classic sheep-farming country for centuries; a Swaledale ram ('tup') is the National Park's symbol. The sheep range onto the fellsides, while cattle are kept in the valleys, providing milk for the famous Wensleydale cheese.

Recently mechanization and an increase in cattle numbers have encouraged a move away from traditional farming. Ancient hay meadows, rich in wildflowers and cut once annually, have given way to 'improved' grassland, where reseeding with quick-growing, fertilized ryegrass allows farmers to take two cuts for silage. Along with land drainage, this has had a damaging effect on wildflowers, birds and wildlife.

Today, tourism is a major source of income: some 15 million people live in cities (such as Leeds and Manchester) within two hours' drive, and summer day-trippers and holidaymakers dwarf the resident population of 20,000. 'Honeypot' areas,

Location: North-west corner of Yorkshire, and a small part of south-east Cumbria.

Climate: Variable, even within one dale. Relatively dry and often warm May–October, but can be bleak on the high fells, with rain and deep snow.

When to Go: Spring and summer for wildflowers, breeding birds, butterflies; walking, climbing and other activities all year.

Access: By car, via M6, then east along A65; or via A1, then westbound, either on A59 Harrogate-Skipton for southern dales, or A684 for western and northern dales; minor roads lead into the heart of the Park and the east. By rail, via the Leeds-Lancaster line (various stations along the south of the Park), or the spectacular Settle-Carlisle line (for stations along its western side). Good network of bus services. The Dales Way, Ribble Way and Pennine Way cross the Park; many footpaths; also circular Yorkshire Dales Cycle Way.

Permits: None required.

Equipment: Waterproofs are advisable.

Facilities: Wide choice of hotels, B&Bs, self-catering accommodation, campsites; 12 youth hostels. There are 7 Park information centres (April-October) and a Field Studies Council centre at Malham Tarn (May-September). NP guided walks.

Watching Wildlife: Good range of upland birds: grouse, waders, birds of prey; and waterbirds. Also deer, Badgers and Foxes.

Visitor Activities: Walking, cycling, caving and potholing, rock climbing, geology, bird-watching, botany, entomology and wildlife pursuits, fishing, canoeing and other watersports.

Above: *The Kingfisher is found along slow-flowing rivers where it can catch small fish such as Minnows; it also needs steep sandy banks in which to dig out its nesting burrow.*

especially Wensleydale and Wharfedale, are particularly popular, as are Malham, Bolton Abbey and Aysgarth Falls; but there are still plenty of opportunities for getting away from it all.

Limestone Country

Britain's finest limestone scenery is found here. Countless frosts and water erosion have carved striking patterns in the great west-east cliffs (scars), forming spectacular examples at Malham Cove, and the Attermire and Gordale Scars.

Above the scars, on the high fell tops, the meagre peaty soil has often been washed away to reveal expanses of limestone 'pavement', with superb examples at Malham Cove, Southerscales Scars and Scales Moor; the Dales contain at least half the limestone pavement in Britain. Over millions of years rainwater has dissected the plateaux into great slabs (clints), separated by deep, narrow fissures (grykes), with stunted trees and lime-loving plantlife.

Underground rivers have created over 50 major caves, more than in the whole of the rest of Britain. Although much of this subterranean world is strictly for experienced cavers, there are show caves at White Scar Caves (the longest in England) at Ingleton and Ingleborough Cave at Clapham, and Stump Cross Caverns, between Grassington and Pateley Bridge. At Ingleborough you can descend on a bosun's chair into nearby Gaping Ghyll – a pothole with a sheer drop of 111 metres (365 feet) – to the 137-metre (450-foot) long main chamber, Britain's biggest underground cavern.

Limestone quarrying – and illegal removal of rock by gardeners – has damaged parts of this splendid natural heritage, and the National Park protects some of the best remaining sites.

Special Plants and Birds

The ancient meadows are bright with buttercups and wildflowers in spring and early summer, while Cowslips, Mountain Pansies and Bird's-eye Primroses grow on the higher pastures. In the remaining pockets of Ash and Hazel woodland are Guelder Rose, Primrose, Globeflower, Baneberry and Wood Crane's-bill, and birds such as Woodcock, Sparrowhawk, Wood Warbler and Redstart. In many woods there are Badgers, and Foxes are common.

On the drier, eastern, side are expanses of heather moorland – Britain's finest grouse moors – managed for the Red Grouse, the main quarry of those who pay highly for shooting rights. Black Grouse have declined alarmingly in recent years.

Waders breed on the wet, rushy grassland on the higher western fells: Curlews, Golden Plover, Lapwings, Snipe and Redshank. Birds of prey on the moors include Short-eared Owls, Merlins and Peregrines. Smaller upland birds include Meadow Pipits, and Skylarks, which have declined in recent years, and summer-visiting Wheatears and Ring Ouzels, returning from Africa as early as March.

Wildlife by the Water

The Dales rivers are fed by many clear rushing streams (becks). The area is renowned for rapids and waterfalls, such as the 27-metre (90-foot) Hardraw Force in Wensleydale. The watercourses attract a variety of birds, notably Grey Herons, Common Sandpipers, Dippers, Grey Wagtails and Kingfishers, while the damp meadows are graced by summer-visiting species such as Yellow Wagtails and Oystercatchers.

Right: *Hardraw Force is England's highest waterfall.*

Below: *The natural amphitheatre of Malham Cove attracts hosts of visitors, but a weekday visit outside the summer season should prove quieter.*

THE LAKE DISTRICT NATIONAL PARK

Land of Harmony and Contrast

Location: Occupies the south-west third of the county of Cumbria, north-west England.

Climate: The central fells are the wettest part of Britain, with frequent rain and mist; but the weather is very changeable and the sun may suddenly break through. Proper preparation and sensible precautions vital when walking on the fells.

When to Go: Any time of year will bring delights, from the spring flowers and bird song to the grandeur of the snow-clad fells in winter.

Access: By road, from the M6, take exit 36 or 37 for Kendal and the southern lakes, or exit 40 for Keswick and the north. By rail, main-line London–Glasgow trains stop at Oxenholme (local trains to Windermere), Penrith and Carlisle. Good network of local buses.

Permits: None required.

Equipment: Fleece and water-proofs can be required on the fells all year.

Facilities: Plenty of hotels and B&Bs in the towns; self-catering cottages, farmhouse B&Bs, camp and caravan sites, and youth hostels. Many NP and Cumbria Tourist Board information points.

Watching Wildlife: Good range of moorland and mountain animals and plants, and a rich variety of wildlife in the woods and along the rivers and streams; most birds on the lakes and smaller meres and tarns in winter, including Goldeneye and other ducks, Whooper Swans and huge gull roosts.

Visitor Activities: Walking, climbing, cycling, riding, fishing, bird-watching, botany, entomology and general natural history.

The Lake District (often referred to simply as Lakeland) has some of the finest scenery in Europe. This is Britain's largest National Park, with an area of 2,292 square kilometres (885 square miles). However, as it is only 51 kilometres (32 miles) across, its many high mountains and deep lakes are closely packed together, giving the landscape a drama out of all proportion to its scale. With annual visitor figures today of 12 million, its beauty has been appreciated by travellers for almost 200 years, largely since the late 18th and early 19th century Romantic movement, and especially through the writings of the famous local poet William Wordsworth and the other so-called Lake Poets, and painters such as J.M.W. Turner. Lakeland was the adopted home of Beatrix Potter, writer and illustrator of the classic series of children's books featuring Peter Rabbit. She left her extensive estate to the National Trust, who safeguard it today, along with many other sites.

As well as having England's longest and deepest lakes, the Lake District contains the country's

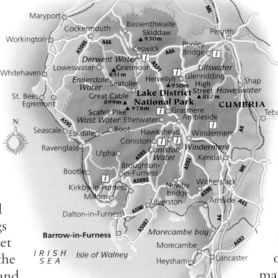

Top left: *A winter scene at Ullswater.*

Opposite, top: *The dramatic landscape is heightened by the frequent contrast between darkness and light, seen here at the southern end of Derwentwater.*

Opposite, bottom left: *The Red Squirrel still thrives in Lakeland woods.*

Opposite, bottom right: *A juvenile Peregrine Falcon clutches its prey.*

greatest mountains: Scafell Pike, the highest (978 metres/3,210 feet); Scafell (964 metres/3,162 feet); Helvellyn (950 metres/3,118 feet); Skiddaw (930 metres/3,053 feet); and Great Gable (899 metres/2,949 feet).

The National Park is immensely rich in wildlife, geology, archaeology and history, and contains no less than 8 NNRs, 120 SSSIs, 82 Regionally Important Geological/ Geomorphological Sites, 1,731 listed buildings and churches and some 200 scheduled ancient monuments.

The 500-million-year-old rocks that make up the impressive scenery of the Lake District are among the oldest in the world. Three main types – Skiddaw Slates, Silurian and Borrowdale Volcanics – make up most of the uplands, producing different soils and vegetation. A bird's-eye view reveals a pattern of deep glacial valleys radiating outwards from the central dome of mountains like the spokes of a giant wheel, interspersed with narrow ridges and sharp peaks. In many of these valleys river water has become dammed behind moraines – huge banks of glacial rubble – to form the deep lakes.

The Fells and Dales

As elsewhere in northern England, the mountains, hills and expanses of upland moor are still known by the name of 'fells', from the Old Norse word *fjall*. This ancient Scandinavian language, spoken by the Viking invaders a thousand years ago, gave the Lake District many of its dialect words and place names: these include '-thwaite', a clearing; 'tarn', from the Norse *tjorn*, a small mountain lake

or pool; 'dale', *dalr*, a valley; 'beck', *bekkr*, a stream, and 'force', *foss*, a waterfall.

The central area of fells is the wettest part of Britain, with an average annual rainfall of 437 centimetres (172 inches). The weather can be dispiriting, with rain and mist blanketing out the scenery for days on end, but it is typically very changeable, with shafts of golden sunlight suddenly brightening an otherwise depressing scene.

This is superb country for walkers and climbers of all levels of expertise, but remember that it is essential to take sensible precautions when up on the fells; several people are killed each year, more than in any other British National Park.

The high mountains are still remote enough to have thriving populations of Ravens. Peregrines are often seen, while Buzzards are abundant. The crags at the head of the Haweswater valley hold England's only nesting Golden Eagles: a pair, sometimes two pairs, have bred – or attempted to do so – each year since the species returned in the late 1960s, after a 180-year absence. They should be watched from the RSPB observation post at Riggindale (April–end August). Like the Ravens, they depend greatly on sheep carrion for survival, especially in lean winter months.

Lower down on the fellsides there are Ring Ouzels and commoner Kestrels, Meadow Pipits, Carrion Crows and Jackdaws. The huge network of meandering drystone walls provides shelter, nest sites and insect food for hole-nesting birds such as Wheatears and Pied Wagtails.

Running Water

One of the most evocative sounds here is that of the many mountain streams, or becks, tumbling down the fellsides. Few animals are able to live in these fast-flowing, ice-cold waters, but Common Sandpipers, Grey Wagtails and Dippers breed along streams and rivers, and by some of the lakes.

Particularly beautiful features of Lakeland are its many hanging valleys formed as the glaciers cut off the small valleys of river tributaries. Today

Top: *Traditionally farmed valleys and wild fells provide habitats for a rich mix of wildlife.*

Left: *One of the most common birds that breed in the uplands of Lakeland is the Meadow Pipit.*

Right: *The old stone bridge at Clappersgate near the popular tourist town of Ambleside.*

Above: *The Common Sandpiper breeds by many lakes, rivers and streams in Lakeland.*

the longest (17 kilometres/10½ miles).

These extensive freshwaters are home to various fish, including Pike and Perch in the nutrient-rich lakes, and Brown Trout, Sea Trout and Salmon in the clearer, deeper, less fertile waters. Another, more unusual member of the trout and salmon family is the Arctic Char, eagerly sought by anglers and one of three species that are relicts of the last Ice Age, trapped as the lakes formed. The other two are the Vendace, found only in Derwentwater and Bassenthwaite, and the Skelly (or Schelly), sometimes dubbed the 'freshwater herring', in Haweswater, Ullswater and Red Tarn.

Woodlands

Although much of Lakeland's dense forest has been cleared since prehistoric times, remnants of ancient Oak and Ash woodlands can still be seen on some hillsides and around lakes. There are extensive plantations, largely coniferous, owned mainly by the Forestry Commission, such as Grizedale Forest between Coniston Water and Windermere. Including native Oakwoods, it has abundant wildlife, several excellent nature trails, a visitor centre, and over 80 remarkable stone and wood sculptures created by invited artists.

they are the sites of dramatic waterfalls such as Gillercombe and Taylorgill Force, in Borrowdale.

The Lakes

Lakeland has 17 major lakes and hundreds of smaller meres and tarns. Wastwater is the deepest lake in England (up to 79 metres/258 feet); Windermere is

Red Squirrels, not yet not out-competed by the Grey Squirrels that have replaced them almost everywhere else in England, have one of their few strongholds in Lakeland woods. There are also Foxes, Badgers, deer and small numbers of rare Pine Martens.

Birds include Woodcocks, Green Woodpeckers, Redstarts and Pied Flycatchers in the broadleaved woods and Long-eared Owls, Crossbills, Redpolls and Siskins among the conifers.

Local Traditions

Most of the land of the National Park is privately owned. The main occupations of its 42,000 inhabitants lie in servicing the huge tourist industry and, to a decreasing extent, in sheep farming. To help maintain traditional farms (many of which have been in the same family for generations) and their beneficial effects on wildlife, the National Trust has purchased almost 100 of them, with over 25,000 Herdwicks. These are tough Lakeland sheep, dating back almost a thousand years, whose grazing keeps the fells neatly crew-cut. The skill of the shepherd is publicly displayed at the annual sheep-dog trials, a popular feature of the region. There are also displays of the art of drystone-wall building.

Foxes are still hunted by farmers in traditional Lakeland style, on foot rather than on horseback. Other traditional pursuits include a local form of wrestling, and one of the toughest sports in Britain, fell running, in which the object is to run against competitors for many miles and scale a certain number of peaks in a given time.

Above: *The Golden Eagle breeds – or attempts to do so – in Haweswater each year.*

Below: *Wild country at Hardknott Pass.*

NORTH YORK MOORS NATIONAL PARK

Magnificent Heather Moorland

Location: Lying to the north-east of York, north and west of Scarborough, south of Teesside.

Climate: Spring/summer fine, warm and sunny; cold winters, with bleak conditions and heavy snow at times on the moor.

When to Go: Spring/summer for breeding birds, wildflowers and butterflies; August–September for heather; all year for general natural history, walking and other activities.

Access: By road, via A1, A64 and A169 via Malton and Pickering and across east side to Whitby; via A19 along west, then A170, and B1257 or minor roads; further north off A19, A172 and 171 to Whitby. By rail, main line to York, local trains to Thirsk or Northallerton (west), Malton or Scarborough (south and south-east); main line further north to Darlington, local train to Middlesbrough, then local line to Whitby for north and north-east, with link at Grosmont for North Yorkshire Moors steam railway to Pickering; local bus service (including Moorsbus, certain days May–September).

Permits: None required.

Equipment: Waterproofs are advisable.

Facilities: Hotels, self-catering accommodation, B&Bs, camp/caravan sites; 5 youth hostels.

Watching Wildlife: Many moorland birds and coastal and river birds; deer in woods, Grey and Common Seals; moths, butterflies, reptiles; wildflowers.

Visitor Activities: Walking, riding, cycling, birdwatching, botany and other natural history, sailing and other watersports, fishing.

The 1,436 square kilometres (554 square miles) of the North York Moors National Park, established in 1952, contains the largest expanse of continuous heather moorland in England. Despite its apparent wildness this is essentially a manmade habitat, created by the Bronze Age clearance of dense wildwood, that enabled heather to take over; the heather now covers one-third of the Park.

The local economy depends largely on a combination of tourism, sheep farming and grouse shooting. Some 140 flocks – about 60,000 animals in total, over twice the area's human population – graze the moor. Their steady munching helps to maintain the heather for the grouse that thrive on its young shoots, and also for the tourists who enjoy the most splendid display in August and September, when honey-scented blooms shimmer in the heat haze like a great purple lake as far as the eye can see.

This glorious natural carpet consists of three species: Bell Heather, with deep purple blooms; the pale-pink-flowered, damp-loving Cross-leaved

Top left: *The song of the Skylark still graces the North York Moors, but the species is declining alarmingly nationally, probably due to lack of weeds for it to eat on farmland in winter.*

Opposite: *Wild Daffodils bloom by the River Dove at Farndale. Visitors flock to enjoy this beautiful natural spectacle each spring.*

Heath; and the most abundant, Heather or Ling, whose flowers are pink and purple. Other moorland plants include Crowberry, Bilberry and various sedges, grasses and mosses, and many lichens. Animal life includes Foxes, Slow-worms and day-flying Emperor Moths, whose caterpillars feast on the heather.

As well as the wary Red Grouse, startling walkers as it springs up with its loud 'go-back' calls, the moors also hold Meadow Pipits, Skylarks, and the Merlin, Britain's smallest bird of prey. These are joined in spring by breeding waders – Golden Plovers, Lapwings and Redshanks – and Ring Ouzels. A few Dotterels on migration turn up at traditional stopover sites between late April and late May.

Geological Influences

The Park has a very varied geology. In most places the predominant rock is sandstone, but there is also some limestone, supporting an impressive range of wildflowers. These include arctic-alpine species at their southern limit in Britain, such as low-growing Dwarf Cornel, with its dense purple flowerheads surrounded by four, large petal-like bracts, followed by glowing red berries, and the delicate Chickweed Wintergreen, with star-shaped white flowers. These and many other plants and animals can be found at Levisham Moor Nature Reserve, reached by footpath from Levisham station on the splendid North York Moors steam railway.

This is superb walking country, with more than 1,000 miles (1,600 kilometres) of footpaths, bridlepaths, and ancient packhorse paths. There are

Above: *This typical North York Moors view is across Farndale.*

Right: *The male Emperor Moth, with his feathery antennae, flies fast over the heather in April and May; the larger females are active only at night, though they may sun themselves on warm days.*

Opposite, top: *Controlled burning maintains the health of the heather moorland.*

Opposite, bottom: *Snow can lie for months in winter, creating a landscape of great beauty.*

three long-distance footpaths: the Cleveland Way runs north from the attractive little town of Helmsley, in the Park's south-west corner, across the Hambleton Hills (the western boundary), then swings round to the east and north across the Cleveland Hills before continuing to the coast, where it turns southwards to end at Filey, south of Scarborough. From there it is possible to follow a path via the Tabular Hills along the southern boundary to return to Helmsley, completing a great circle. The other two long-distance paths, the Lyke Wake Walk and Coast-to-coast Walk, run from the Cleveland Hills to the coast.

Varied Habitats

From the flat tops and high ridges of the wild and remote rolling hills there are stunning views across a patchwork of moorland, farmed dales and woodlands. The Park is notable for its great variety of habitats, which enable a correspondingly wide range of wildlife to flourish. About one-fifth of its area is covered by forestry plantations. Their great expanses are not the gloomy, forbidding places they used to be; more wildlife-sensitive management has produced a mixture of stands of different ages, increasing both their scenic value and their appeal

to wildlife. This includes Sparrowhawks, Tawny Owls, Nightjars, Siskins and Crossbills, as well as Roe Deer, with some Fallow and Red Deer.

Deep, narrow valleys cut into the steep slopes of soft limestone of the Tabular Hills in the south: Farndale, Bransdale, Rosedale and Westerdale. Pockets of native deciduous woodland bring further variety to the wildlife. Farndale, an SSSI managed by the Park Authority, is famous for its spectacular spring display of wild Daffodils, while Forge Valley Woods NNR has an excellent range of woodland plants, birds, mammals and other wildlife.

Most of the Park's streams and rivers wind along the secluded dales, their banks rich in wildlife such as Grey Herons, Kingfishers, Grey Wagtails, dragonflies and damselflies. In the north-east corner of the Park, Scaling Dam Reservoir, including a small nature reserve, is one of the best sites for birdwatching, attracting many waterfowl, waders, gulls and other birds; the surrounding moorland is noted for birds of prey in winter, including Hen Harriers, Sparrowhawks, Peregrines, Merlins and Rough-legged Buzzards.

Dramatic Coastline

The North Sea coast forms the Park's eastern boundary, fronted by an impressive series of cliffs. In places, steep wooded valleys ('cloughs') run down

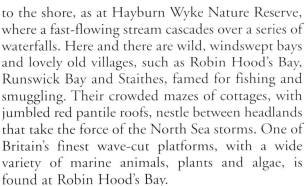

to the shore, as at Hayburn Wyke Nature Reserve, where a fast-flowing stream cascades over a series of waterfalls. Here and there are wild, windswept bays and lovely old villages, such as Robin Hood's Bay, Runswick Bay and Staithes, famed for fishing and smuggling. Their crowded mazes of cottages, with jumbled red pantile roofs, nestle between headlands that take the force of the North Sea storms. One of Britain's finest wave-cut platforms, with a wide variety of marine animals, plants and algae, is found at Robin Hood's Bay.

In the north lies the ancient harbour town of Whitby, with its history of herring fishing and whaling. Today it thrives on tourism; its narrow, winding streets, old houses and shops rise on either side of the river, linked by an old swing bridge, overlooked by the ruins of the 13th-century abbey. Whitby makes a good base for exploring, though it can be unbearably crowded in summer. Many are drawn by its connection with the vampire myth created by the Irish writer Bram Stoker's famous novel *Dracula*, partly set in the town. It is also famous for its links with the great explorer Captain Cook, a north Yorkshireman whose four ships of discovery were all built in Whitby.

Further north at Boulby are the second highest cliffs in England, rising to over 150 metres (500 feet). The area holds impressive colonies of Kittiwakes and Fulmars, and is the site of the only potash mine in the United Kingdom.

NORTHUMBERLAND NATIONAL PARK & THE FARNES

Lonely Hills and Bird-thronged Islands

Extending from the Roman ramparts of Hadrian's Wall in the south to the Cheviot Hills on the Scottish border, Northumberland National Park is the remotest and most northerly of all. Designated in 1956, it covers an area of 1,049 square kilometres (405 square miles) and occupies almost a quarter of the county whose name it bears.

For 300 years until the 16th century, this wild landscape of hills and dales was controlled by border clans (reivers) who took advantage of the Anglo-Scottish hostility to carry out cross-border sheep and cattle rustling and other illegal activities. Today, the only evidence of such events are the 'peels' (defensive towers) and 'bastles' (fortified farmhouses) whose ruins are scattered across the rolling, open landscape, the remotest, loneliest area in England, with a sparse human population.

This is superb walking country, with great open skies and splendid views. The Pennine Way long-distance footpath enters the Park at Hadrian's Wall and leads northwards along the edge of the vast Border Forest Park, then via the attractive town of Bellingham on the North Tyne river to the Cheviot Hills. There, a brief detour reaches the summit of

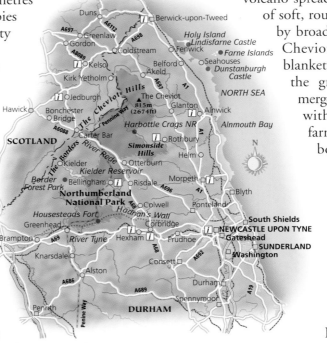

Top left: *Cowslips: a delight in chalk grassland.*

Opposite, top: *Seabird colony on Staple Island.*

Opposite, bottom: *The Longstone Lighthouse.*

The Cheviot, the highest peak at 815 metres (2,674 feet), before crossing the Scottish border to end at the village of Kirk Yetholm.

From the granite summit of The Cheviot, the remains of lava flows from an ancient volcano spread out in a great ring of soft, rounded hills, dissected by broad glacial valleys. The Cheviots are capped by blanket bog, giving way to the grass moorland that merges on the lower slopes with the stone-walled farmland of the valley bottoms, and small pockets of relict native broadleaved woodland. Wildlife includes the abundant Meadow Pipit and scarcer upland birds such as Ring Ouzel and Merlin, with Snipe, Dunlin, and Golden Plover in boggy areas. The Simonside Hills and Harbottle Crags, in the Park's centre, are based on softer, more easily eroded sandstone and have sharper profiles. Largely covered with dark heather moorland, with bracken on the lower slopes, much of the area is managed for grouse shooting. This is one of the best places in Britain for seeing the wary Red Grouse, especially during late winter and spring.

To the west of the Simonside Hills lies the Otterburn army training area, out of bounds for much of the year, with forbidden areas dotted with signs and red flags to warn of live firing.

In the south is the softer landscape of the North Tyne and Rede valleys. Their upper slopes, too, were once clothed with moorland, but much of this

Above: *The Red Grouse breeds on heather moorland and is particularly noticeable in late winter and spring, when the males display and compete for females, accompanied by loud, harsh 'go-back' calls.*

is now covered with a vast area of conifers, forming the largest manmade forest in Britain. Several areas lie just outside the Park: Kielder Forest, Wark Forest, Falstone Forest and Redesdale Forest, together known as the Border Forest Park. The Park skirts the eastern edge of Kielder Forest, within which lies Kielder Water, the biggest reservoir in Western Europe.

Not far away, Hadrian's Wall is well worth a visit: built by the Romans AD 122–126, it was finally abandoned in the late 4th century. The impressive remains include 16 major defensive forts strung out along the wall, interspersed with smaller fortifications.

Small, shallow glacial lakes, or loughs, are scattered throughout the Park. Some, such as Grindon Lough, with open water, attract winter-visiting Whooper Swans, Greylag Geese, and Goosanders and other ducks. Others have become filled in to form mires, holding a rich variety of aquatic plants. Numerous streams also grace the park, tumbling down from the hills via torrents and waterfalls. These provide habitats for a wide range of water-loving plants, freshwater invertebrates, and birds such as Grey Heron, Common Sandpiper, Kingfisher, Grey Wagtail and Dipper, as well as Salmon and Otters.

Right: *A breeding colony of Puffins in July on Staple Island in the Farnes. These attractive and comical birds allow close views.*

The Farne Islands

The shoreline from Cresswell in the south to Berwick-upon-Tweed on the Scottish border is designated as the North Northumberland Heritage Coast: a quiet, often deserted, stretch of sandy bays, dunes and low rocky headlands, dotted with splendidly atmospheric castles.

The rocky, treeless Farne Islands, owned by the National Trust and protected as a NNR, lie 5 kilometres (3 miles) north-east of the small fishing port of Seahouses. These are the easternmost outcrops of the Great Whin Sill, a narrow volcanic intrusion of hard dolerite rock that runs across the north of England and forms the foundation for Hadrian's Wall and Holy Island.

About 70,000 pairs of seabirds breed here; by early August there may be more than 200,000 individuals. These include over 15,000 pairs of Guillemots, which have bred here since at least the 1600s, and some 35,000 pairs of Puffins, as well as Razorbills, Fulmars, Shags and Cormorants, with great numbers of Kittiwakes and other gulls. Also unmissable among the low, grassy, flower-strewn vegetation are the colonies of several thousand Arctic Terns, especially as they have the habit of diving at the heads of unwary visitors. There are similar numbers of Sandwich Terns, a few hundred pairs of Common Terns and the occasional Roseate Tern.

Large numbers of Eider Ducks nest on the islands, their local name, 'Cuddie Ducks', commemorating St Cuthbert, the 7th-century Celtic Bishop of Lindisfarne, who retreated to the islands as a hermit and gave the birds and other wildlife the blessing of his protection, so creating one of the world's earliest nature reserves.

The Farnes' other great wildlife attractions are the Grey Seals from the local breeding colony that bask on the rocks or bob out of the water to gaze at passing boatloads of visitors. Landing is permitted on Longstone, Staple and Inner Farne islands, but the weather or tides can prevent the trip.

Holy Island

Less than 8 kilometres (5 miles) north of the Farnes lies the low hump of Holy Island, also known as Lindisfarne (that name is also used for the NNR that includes Budle Bay and the adjacent stretch of coastline). This is a magical place, with its imposing 16th-century castle set atop a rocky outcrop, and 7th-century priory where the holy relics of St Cuthbert were originally buried, making it a place of pilgrimage for centuries.

Lindisfarne's sand dunes and damp hollows ('slacks') are home to a wealth of wildflowers, such as Cowslips, Grass of Parnassus, Bog Pimpernel and various orchids.

This is also a splendid place for the birdwatcher, and is the main British site for the pale-bellied race of the Brent Goose, which breeds on the Arctic island of Svalbard and migrates here for the winter.

Above: *Looking east along Hadrian's Wall towards Housesteads Fort.*

Below: *Scarcest by far of the regular British breeding terns, the Roseate Tern, seen here at Inner Farne Island.*

WALES

COVERING 20,780 SQUARE KILOMETRES (8,023 square miles), Wales is surrounded by sea on three sides, its eastern flanks forming the border with England. This beautiful country has a greater variety of landscapes than any other similarly sized region in the British Isles, and is the wildest part of southern Britain. Apart from concentrations of population in the old mining valleys of the south-east and along the north coast, Wales is sparsely populated.

Over half the country lies over 168 metres (550 feet) above sea level: nowhere else in the British Isles is there such a concentration of mountains and hills in so small an area. There

are two major mountain regions: Snowdonia, with stunning scenery and the highest peaks in the British Isles outside Scotland, and further south the more modest but equally wild Black Mountains and Brecon Beacons.

These are linked by the country's backbone, the Cambrian Mountains, containing some of Wales' wildest and loveliest landscapes. They are havens for wildlife, with rare species such as Red Kites and Polecats. There are also other beautiful hills, such as the Clwydian Range in the north-east and the Preseli Hills in the south-west.

Almost 20 per cent of Wales lies within its three National Parks: Snowdonia, the largest and most varied, famed for rock climbing and glacial landscapes, with a huge range of habitats and wildlife; Brecon Beacons, with its lonely moorlands, bleak peaks, glass-clear lakes and huge cave systems; and the Pembrokeshire Coast, including not only one of Britain's finest stretches of coastline, but also some of its best seabird islands, large Grey Seal colonies and a wealth of marine life, including dolphins, porpoises and Basking Sharks.

Opposite left: *Thrift, which is usually pink as shown here, is a very typical coastal flower.*

Below: *The Snowdonia National Park is one of Britain's finest National Parks, with superb walking, climbing and wildlife to enjoy amid magnificent scenery, as here, looking west towards Snowdon, the highest peak in Wales.*

PEMBROKESHIRE COAST NATIONAL PARK

Spectacular Coasts and Islands

With an area of 620 square kilometres (240 square miles), this is the smallest National Park (established in 1952), and the only one that is predominantly coastal. It contains a tremendous range of landscapes for its size. As well as offshore islands, sea cliffs, sandy beaches and dunes, muddy estuaries and saltmarsh, it includes heathland, hills, woodlands, rivers and lakes. It has one of the highest densities of protected environmental sites in Europe.

This is an ancient landscape of great geological interest, borne on the oldest rocks in Wales, dating back some 600 million years. There is much of historical interest, with extensive evidence of prehistoric peoples, including burial chambers and standing stones. More recent history is represented by the castles at Manorbier, Carew and Pembroke.

Rugged Coastline

Walking along the spectacular 299-kilometre/186-mile long Pembrokeshire Coast Path, running from Amroth in the south to St Dogmael's in the north, is the best way to enjoy the Park.

Top left: *Looking along the low cliffs of Skokholm island towards the lighthouse.*

Opposite, top: *Skokholm Bird Observatory.*

Opposite, bottom: *Ramsons (Wild Garlic) in woodland at Stackpole National Nature Reserve.*

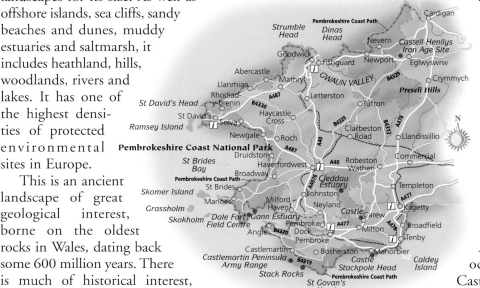

Pembrokeshire Coast National Park

Stackpole National Nature Reserve, on the south coast, has duneland and chalk grassland plants, as well as mature woodlands. The elongated Bosherston Lakes created by the damming of three narrow limestone valleys between 1780 and 1840 have Otters, wintering wildfowl and over 20 species of dragonflies and damselflies. Stackpole Head has large colonies of breeding Guillemots and Razorbills, while just to the west Stack Rocks (Elegug Stacks) is one of the best places in the British Isles to see cliff-nesting seabirds at close range. Access across the Army tank range (which occupies most of the Castlemartin peninsula) is restricted.

Wild St David's Head has the finest area of coastal heathland in Britain, with many scarce plants and insects and rich Neolithic and Iron Age remains, while Strumble Head to the north is one of the world's finest sites for watching seabird migration.

The clifftop grasslands and heaths contain a great variety of plants and invertebrates, and are vitally important feeding grounds for Choughs, the British Isles' rarest species of crow.

Harbour of Contrasts

Away from the incongruous noise and artificial lights of the great complex of oil refineries, the mudflats and saltmarshes of the Milford Haven creeks and the long, secluded estuaries of the Gann and the Cleddau rivers are important sites

Above: *As well as having dramatic cliffs and winding estuaries, the Pembrokeshire coast also includes many beautiful, unspoilt sandy bays.*

Opposite, top: *The cathedral at St David's towers over the little town, the smallest cathedral city in the British Isles. It was founded by St David, patron saint of Wales, in the 6th century, and rebuilt between 1180 and 1522.*

Opposite, centre: *Visitors to Skomer disembark from the boat at Martin's Haven, on the mainland opposite.*

Opposite, bottom: *A Manx Shearwater returns to its nest burrow on Skokholm under cover of darkness to avoid predators.*

for wildfowl and waders, especially in winter. In their upper reaches, feeding sites are protected within the Cleddau/Daugleddau Wildfowl Sanctuary.

The Preseli Hills

In the north, the National Park extends far inland, and includes Mynydd (or Bryniau) Preseli. The final southern outliers of the Cambrian Mountain chain that runs the length of Wales, they climb abruptly to a maximum height of 536 metres (1,759 feet) at Foel Cwmcerwyn.

Preseli was the source of many of the inner standing stones, or megaliths, raised about 1675BC at Britain's most famous prehistoric monument: Stonehenge, on Salisbury Plain, Wiltshire. It must have been an astonishing feat for people living over 3,500 years ago to hew and transport the great slabs of bluestone, each weighing about four tonnes, over more than 320 kilometres (200 miles). Mynydd Preseli is the only known place in Britain where this bluestone – spotted dolerite, rhyolite and volcanic ash – is found.

The Pembrokeshire Islands

The islands off Pembrokeshire's west coast are internationally important for their seabird and seal populations; all are SSSIs and a Special Protection Area under the EC Directive on the Conservation of Wild Birds. The foreshore and the sea surrounding Skomer, together with those of the mainland opposite, are protected as one of only two statutory Marine Nature Reserves in the UK. A visit to any of them brings a good chance of seeing Harbour

Porpoises (and sometimes Common and Risso's Dolphins), and huge Basking Sharks and Sunfish.

The northernmost, Ramsey, lies less than 1.6 kilometre (1 mile) from the mainland, across a turbulent channel known as The Bitches. It towers up to 137 metres (450 feet) above the high western cliffs. Protected as an RSPB reserve, NNR, SSSI and Geological Conservation Review Site, it is a breeding stronghold for Choughs, with a few pairs of Lapwings, declining alarmingly elsewhere.

Skomer (almost 302 hectares/745 acres with the islet of Middleholm to its east) is the largest, with varied rocks and cliffs. Huge seabird citadels fill many of the cliff ledges in spring and early summer, producing a cacophony of calls from Guillemots, Razorbills, Kittiwakes and other gulls, and Fulmars. In spring there are great drifts of wildflowers: pink Thrift, Red Campion, white Sea Campion, Bluebells and yellow Primroses. All the islands hold large numbers of rabbits, and Skomer also has the unique Skomer Vole, a larger race of the mainland Bank Vole.

Skokholm, with low red sandstone cliffs differing from the volcanic rocks of the other islands, is more exposed and covers only 98 hectares (242 acres). The famous naturalist and island-lover R.M.Lockley started his pioneering studies of seabirds and rabbits after he settled there in 1927, establishing Britain's first bird observatory in 1933. Rabbit burrows riddle the entire island, providing nesting sites for Puffins and Manx Shearwaters, the most numerous seabirds on Skomer too. By day you can walk among throngs of comical, colourful

Puffins; on moonless nights you can listen to thousands of Manx Shearwaters as they return to their burrows on the islands, using the cloak of darkness to avoid predatory Great Black-backed Gulls. Skomer holds the world's largest colonies with over 100,000 pairs. From August, the adults leave on their annual migration to South America, 8,000 kilometres (5,000 miles) away. Smaller numbers of tiny Storm-petrels nest in rocky crevices as well as in burrows, returning at night to sing their strange, guttural purring songs.

These islands are superb places for observing migration of landbirds as well as seabirds, with rarities recorded annually. On Skokholm, there is a tradition that whenever someone finds a new bird, they paint it on a wall at the visitor centre.

The largest breeding herd of Grey Seals in southern Britain can be found on Ramsey, and the second largest on Skomer. Several hundred pups are born each autumn.

Grassholm lies 11.3 kilometres (7 miles) off-shore. Owned by the RSPB, and a NNR, this bare, flat-topped island holds the world's fourth largest colony of Gannets, with 33,000 breeding pairs. These dazzling white seabirds with black-tipped wings spanning 1.8 metres (6 feet) numbered only 20 pairs in 1860. The colony covers much of the little island's 9 hectares (22 acres), and it is no longer possible to land there. A boat trip round the island guarantees a spectacular view, as well as the birds' massed groans, barks and croaks – and the smell of their droppings! Gannets can often be seen plummeting into the sea to catch fish.

GOWER PENINSULA

Unspoilt Corner of South Wales

Location: Extending into the Bristol Channel from the south Wales coast, west of Swansea.

Climate: Mild; fine, warm, summer weather; can be very windy along coasts and on open higher ground in centre of peninsula.

When to Go: Spring and summer best for wildflowers/butterflies.

Access: By car, from Swansea via A4118 across southern Gower to Port Eynon, from where B4247 continues to Rhossili. In the north, B4271/B4295 to Llanrhidian, then by minor roads. Regular bus services from Swansea.

Permits: Not required. Restrictions on entry to parts of some reserves e.g. Oxwich in bird breeding season or to protect dunes and vegetation. Worm's Head accessible for only 2½ hours at low tide (dangerous at other times), its seabird colony is out of bounds from March–July.

Equipment: Waterproofs are advisable.

Facilities: Plenty of hotels in Swansea, including Mumbles, and west towards Caswell Bay; B&Bs, camp and caravan sites in various parts of the peninsula. NT visitor information centre at Rhossili. Organized walks by Glamorgan Wildlife Trust and Countryside Council for Wales.

Watching Wildlife: Great for botanists, especially the limestone grasslands of south-coast clifftops. Rich insect fauna includes Great Green Bushcricket and many butterflies, including Marbled White. Many seabirds along south coast; wildfowl and waders on the north coast; area renowned for marine biology.

Visitor Activities: Botany, entomology, birdwatching, marine biology, walking, cycling, rock climbing, sea fishing.

This gem of a place provides a rural playground for those from the urban areas of South Wales, and for holidaymakers from further afield. Extending into the Bristol Channel immediately to the west of Swansea, the Gower (Welsh: *Gwyr*) is a small peninsula, less than 32 kilometres (20 miles) long and barely 8 kilometres (5 miles) wide. Its narrow lanes and beauty spots can become crowded in summer, and it is popular with surfers and hang-gliders, but you can always escape from the hordes, and it is much quieter out of season. Few roads reach the sea, but there is a good network of coastal paths.

Along Gower's popular south coast you can explore a series of beautiful bays and rocky headlands, with stunning clifftop views and plenty of opportunities for beachcombers and rock-pool explorers. In many places the rocks are honeycombed with the tunnels of boring sponges and worms and spattered with a variety of lichens, which thrive in the relatively unpolluted air. Erosion has resulted in many sea caves.

The limestone grasslands of the clifftops feature uncommon wildflowers such as White and Hoary Rock Roses, Small Scabious, Clary, Spring Cinquefoil and Yellow Whitlowgrass, the last-named unique to the Gower.

Top left: *Turnstones, such as this juvenile bird, can be seen along rocky shores all round Gower.*

Opposite, top: *The huge sweep of Rhossili Bay.*

Opposite, bottom: *The reedbeds at Oxwich NNR are among the largest in south-west Britain.*

Eastern Gower

The eastern fringes of the peninsula are largely built up, though the old pier at Mumbles holds a thriving breeding colony of Kittiwakes, and Mumbles Head is a good site for observing seabird migration. The name of this Swansea suburb derives from the French *mamelles* (breasts), referring to the twin islets lying just offshore.

Moving westwards, Caswell and Langland Bays are often crowded, though tiny Brandy Cove and Pwlldu Bay are unreachable by road and worth visiting. Three Cliffs Bay is one of the most perfect stretches of shoreline in the whole of Britain, bordered by the graceful sweep of cliffs ending in the three sharp masses that give it its name.

Oxwich Bay

Further west, the 289-hectare (714-acre) Oxwich NNR has a wide variety of habitats. The 4-kilometre (2.5-mile) long, shallow bay is backed by a fine dune system, developed over some 2,500 years, behind which lies a large area of saltmarshes, freshwater marshes and fens, with artificial fish ponds.

The dunes provide a superb example of classic vegetational succession, and a nature trail takes the visitor from the embryonic dunes on the beach, where plants such as Prickly Saltwort and Sea Holly trap wind-blown sand, through areas of Marram Grass on to the mature dunes, with Sea Bindweed, Evening Primrose and Ragwort (between which there are damp 'slacks', where orchids thrive), and finally plant-filled meadowland. There are over 600 species of flowering plants, including rarities such as Dune Gentian.

Above: *Along with the commoner Turnstones, Purple Sandpipers may be seen on rocky shores. Because they occur in small numbers spread over many miles of shoreline, they are often overlooked.*

Below: *Burry Inlet, on Gower's northern coast, is a peaceful, little visited haven where wildfowl and waders abound on the huge area of mudflats and one of Britain's largest areas of saltmarsh.*

Among the marshes and fens are many dragonflies and damselflies, as well as Common Frogs, Smooth Newts, and a good range of aquatic plants. The reedbeds have healthy populations of Reed and Sedge Warblers and a few Cetti's Warblers, as well as Water Rails. Marsh Harriers and Kingfishers stop by in autumn, and Bitterns are annual winter visitors.

Port Eynon to Rhossili and Worm's Head

Walking the clifftop path between Port Eynon and Rhossili is an exhilarating experience: the rock here has tilted, folded, faulted and eroded into an extraordinary variety of shapes. The wildflowers are superb, and there is a chance of seeing a Chough, as the species returned here to breed in 1991, for the first time this century. The walk passes through six Glamorgan Wildlife Trust nature reserves, and also by Paviland (or Goat's Hole) Cave, where the partial skeleton of the 'Red Lady of Paviland' was uncovered in 1823, along with pieces of a mammoth skull. It turned out to belong to a male Palaeolithic hunter, and is at least 19,000 years old.

Rhossili Down, at the southern end of Rhossili Bay, is a great whaleback ridge of grass, shrubby heathland and boggy hollows, good for insects and migrant birds. Looking out to sea here you will see the narrow promontory known as Worm's Head ('The Worm'). This can be reached for about five hours each day, during low to mid tide, across a rocky causeway frequented by Turnstones and, in autumn and winter, by Purple Sandpipers. Rare plants grow on the steep, south-facing slopes where Rock Pipits nest, and the cliffs of the outer head have the only sizeable mixed colony of breeding seabirds in south-east Wales. Access to the cliffs is discouraged from mid-March to July.

North Gower

A lonely region of flat marshes, mudflats and sandbanks with little access by car, Gower's north coast has far fewer visitors. It overlooks Burry Inlet, which includes the largest area of saltmarsh in Wales, and is favoured by many waders and wildfowl. Also known as the Loughor Estuary, it is famed for Cockles, which once provided employment for many local women who, accompanied by donkeys to carry their catches, raked the Llanrhidian Sands. Today, cockle-fishing is on a far smaller scale, but there are still plenty of them, relished by Oystercatchers, which occur in large numbers here.

To the west of Llanrhidian Sands lies the huge dune system of Whiteford Burrows, on Berges Island (not actually an island), which extends 3.2 kilometres (2 miles) northwards. Owned by the National Trust, this remote NNR is renowned for its superb wildflowers, including Moonwort, Yellow Bird's-nest and Sea Pansies, its insects, and the birds on the estuary, such as (in winter) Brent Geese, Wigeon and Shelduck. The birds are best seen just after high tide, as the water recedes to expose feeding areas. Eider Duck, far south of their nearest regular breeding sites in northern England and Scotland, occur here all year.

BRECON BEACONS NATIONAL PARK

Wild Uplands and Huge Cave Systems

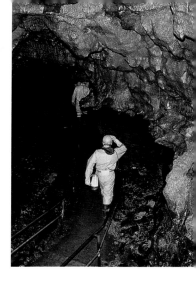

This thinly populated, mainly upland area of south-east Wales, covering an area of 1,344 square kilometres (519 square miles), was declared a National Park in 1957. Old Red Sandstone dominates the landscape, giving the exposed rocky outcrops a range of colours from warm purplish-russet to pale grey-green, though deep burgundy red predominates. By contrast, the southern borders are formed of millstone grit (together with the northern fringes of the coal measures that rendered Glamorgan, to the south, one of the world's greatest coalfields). Between the millstone grit and sandstone are outcrops of Carboniferous limestone around the rivers flowing south from the mountains. Over millions of years, erosion of this soft rock has created dramatic cave systems.

There is a whole range of well-preserved archaeological sites, from the Neolithic, Bronze and Iron Ages through to Roman and Norman times. From the late fifteenth century industries such as coal mining, charcoal burning, limestone quarrying and iron smelting developed in the Park and the surrounding area, leaving behind a rich heritage of industrial archaeology.

Sweeping Mountains

Four great blocks of sandstone mountains, cut through by predominantly north–south river valleys, dominate the Park. In the west lies The Black Mountain (Y Mynydd Du), and in the east the confusingly named Black Mountains on the border with England, which form the largest continuous area of high ground in south Wales. In between lie

Top right: *Entering the Dan-yr-Ogof show caves, claimed to be the largest system in Western Europe.*

the lonely mountains of Fforest Fawr and the Brecon Beacons. To the north lies the west–east Usk valley, and then the Mynydd Epynt, from where the mountains continue north to Snowdonia. The highest point in southern Britain is Pen y Fan at 886 metres/2,907 feet, in the Brecon Beacons. Although they are not the highest in Wales, these are the most southerly 'real' mountains in Britain. They have a distinctive shape, like great waves frozen in time.

Their flanks are covered mainly by smooth, grass-covered sweeps of sheep-grazed moorland: nowadays, heather and Bilberry occupy less than a quarter of the total moorland area. Lower down on the hillsides and in the valley bottoms lies a patchwork of fields bordered by neat hedges, and the whole region is great for walking all year round.

The dramatic escarpment of The Black Mountain climbs to a height of 802 metres (2,631 feet) at Fan Brycheiniog. Its towering red cliffs overlook a beautiful glacial lake, Llyn y fan Fach.

Five scarce species of whitebeams grow in the densely wooded limestone cliffs and screes of the National Nature Reserve of Craig y Ciliau on the northern flank of Mynydd Llangatwg, in the heart of the Brecon Beacons. One of these, the Small-leaved Whitebeam, is found nowhere else in the world. On the high limestone ledges grow Ice Age remnants of alpine and sub-alpine vegetation – Purple and Mossy Saxifrages, Northern Bedstraw, Dwarf Willow and the fern Green Spleenwort – here at their most southerly limit in Britain.

This is a good place to see upland birds in spring and summer, including Red Grouse, Buzzards,

Location: South-east Wales, extending from the Black Mountains on the English border in the east almost 64 km (40 miles) westwards to the mountains of the Carmarthen Van.

Climate: Very changeable weather, particularly on high ground; driving rain, gales, swirling mist and low temperatures possible in midsummer; rainfall high; snow in winter.

When to Go: Any time of year for walker/naturalist; birds/wildflowers best in spring/summer.

Access: By road, to within 32 km (20 miles) of southern boundary via the M4: from exit 26 at Newport, take the A4042 for Pontypool/Abergavenny; from exit 32, follow the A470 for Brecon. By rail, change at Newport for Abergavenny or at Cardiff for Merthyr Tydfil. NP Authority runs sustainable transport Beacons Bus.

Permits: Not required.

Equipment: Fleece and waterproofs can be required all year.

Facilities: Wide variety of accommodation, from hotels and B&Bs to camp and caravan sites within the Park in Brecon, Talgarth, Hay-on-Wye and Crickhowell; just outside in Abergavenny, Merthyr Tydfil, Llandeilo and Llandovery; 5 youth hostels.

Watching Wildlife: Plantlife includes fine woodlands, arctic-alpine flowers in the high mountains and rare aquatic plants at Llangorse Lake; birds include Buzzards (common) and Red Kites, wildfowl on lakes/reservoirs, and riverside species; mammals include Badgers.

Visitor Activities: Walking, horse riding, caving and potholing, canoeing, sailing, cycling, birdwatching, botany, fishing, archaeology, industrial history.

Above: *The Polecat, almost exterminated by gamekeepers and landowners for its fur by the end of the 19th century, has made a comeback in Wales, including the Brecon Beacons.*

The Largest Lake

Llangorse Lake (Llyn Syfaddan) is the largest area of natural freshwater in south Wales. A shallow basin scoured out of the sandstone by an Ice Age glacier and dammed by a gravel barrier, it contains a rich assemblage of aquatic plants, including 25 rare species. They include Yellow, White and Fringed Water-lilies, Greater Spearwort and Golden Dock.

Sadly, despite the lake being made an SSSI in 1954, wildlife here has faced pressures due to pollution by sewage and ongoing nutrient enrichment from farmland, resulting in the loss of some of the scarcer and more specialized aquatic plants and insects. The development of water sports has also been detrimental. Llangorse has long been a prime Welsh breeding site for elegant Great Crested Grebes, but their numbers have dropped dramatically. However, the large reedbeds support good numbers of Reed Warblers, Sedge Warblers, Reed Buntings and Water Rails, and a few Bitterns visit them in most winters.

Even in the coldest weather there is still a good range of wildfowl, including up to 200 Pochard and a similar number of Tufted Duck, with smaller numbers of Wigeon, Mallard, Gadwall, Teal, Shoveler, Goldeneye and Goosander, and occasionally other ducks and Bewick's and Whooper Swans from the Arctic. The lake also holds a wide variety of fish, including Pike, Perch, Roach and Eel.

Underground Attractions

Beneath the limestone crags in the southern part of the Park lies the most extensive cave system in

Peregrine Falcons, Merlins, Wheatears and Ring Ouzels, as well as more numerous Skylarks and Meadow Pipits. Along the many rivers and streams Common Sandpipers, Grey Wagtails and Dippers can be encountered.

In the broadleaved woodlands of the valleys there are carpets of Bluebells in spring, and breeding birds include Redstarts, Pied Flycatchers, various warblers, Nuthatches and Treecreepers, while scarce Polecats – members of the weasel family – are found, much more common in rural Wales than elsewhere in Britain.

Britain. In some areas the ground is pockmarked with hollows (swallow or shake holes): there are more of these per square kilometre than anywhere else in Britain. Rivers and streams roar through gorges and plunge down splendid waterfalls, such as the 30-metre (100-foot) drop at Henrhyd.

Underground rivers have worn away huge caves and extensive passages, with impressive stalagmites and stalactites, home to specialized creatures, including semi-transparent, blind species of crustaceans. They also form vital roost sites for nine species of bat; the Lesser Horseshoe Bat penetrates as far as 4.8 kilometres (3 miles) underground. In prehistoric times, Brown Bears, deer and Aurochs (wild oxen) sheltered in these caves.

Members of caving clubs from all over the world come to explore these outstanding cave systems. Experienced cavers can enjoy the thrill of entering the great cave system of Ogof Ffynnon Ddu, one of Europe's deepest and the only cave NNR in Britain. Others can visit the impressive Dan-yr-Ogof and Cathedral show caves in the Tawe valley.

Right: *The Brecon Beacons are famed for the number and beauty of their waterfalls. The waterfall of Pistyll Rhaeadr is one of the Seven Wonders of Wales.*

Below: *A typical view of the Black Mountains and their surrounding expanse of high ground dotted with grazing sheep.*

SNOWDONIA NATIONAL PARK

Welsh Mountain Fastness

The second largest National Park (after the Lake District), Snowdonia National Park – the first in Wales, established in 1951 – has an area of 2,170 square kilometres (838 square miles). The Welsh name for Snowdonia is Eryri, possibly deriving from the word *eryri* (land of eagles), although evidence suggests that Golden Eagles were probably extinct there by the mid-18th century. Alternative origins lie in *eira* (land of snow) or an old word meaning high place; indeed, snow can lie on the highest peaks as late as May.

There is no doubt that this wild, intensely beautiful region contains some of the most stunning landscapes in the British Isles. Although the mountains may not have the scale and grandeur of the Scottish Highlands, they are packed into a much smaller area, and appear to soar more dramatically into the sky. This superb mountaineering country has been the training ground for many climbers who have conquered major world peaks, including Everest. Although it is perfectly possible to enjoy many of the best views without climbing, visitors should be aware that this can be dangerous

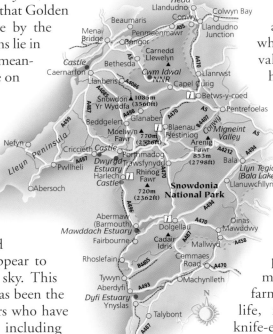

terrain; people die on the mountains every year. At any season the weather can change in an instant, as bright sunlight is replaced by lashing sheets of cold, gusting rain, or great swirling cloaks of mist.

This rugged landscape is the result of glacial action in the last Ice Age, which carved out deep valleys and mountain hollows, or cwms. The intricate foldings and upthrusts of the ancient rocks have created a classic site, visited by early geologists and famed worldwide for its wealth of geomorphological features.

Most of the land is privately owned, and much is given over to hill farming, an immensely hard life, now on an economic knife-edge for those families who continue the tradition of generations. Hardy Welsh Mountain Sheep far outnumber humans here. There are also smaller numbers of cattle, notably tough dual-purpose Welsh Blacks, the occasional herd of feral goats, and wild ponies, which roam the great slopes of the Carneddau.

Remnants of the once-thriving slate industry, which supplied the best roofing slate worldwide and dominated the area economically and socially, are evident, especially around Blaenau Ffestiniog. There are show mines, and tours of the mine workings, including a ride on Britain's steepest underground railway, with an almost 1 in 2 incline. Also in the area is the Ffestiniog narrow-gauge steam railway, and a major hydroelectric scheme. Tourism is the region's main industry today.

Top left: *Superbly preserved rail carriages still carry visitors up to the summit of Snowdon the easy way.*

Opposite, top left: *The Pied Flycatcher is one of the most attractive summer visitors to the oakwoods.*

Opposite, centre left: *The lovely Purple Saxifrage.*

Opposite, bottom left: *Siskins breed mainly in conifer woodlands.*

Opposite, right: *Frost-shattered boulders lie along the lower slopes of the challenging Glyder range.*

Above: *The abandoned workings of the great Dinorwic slate quarry tower up to 600 metres (1,900 feet) above Llyn Peris, near Llanberis. Closed in 1969 after a major rock fall, it now holds the vast subterranean chambers of a hydroelectricity generating station.*

Opposite, bottom: *The Swallow Falls, one of Snowdonia's most famous beauty spots, lies a short way from the small tourist town of Betws-y-Coed.*

Exploring the Mountains

The Snowdon massif is the highest mountain in England and Wales, with its tallest peak – known in Welsh as *Yr Wyddfa* ('the burial place', referring to a now-vanished ancient burial mound) – reaching 1,085 metres (3,560 feet). About 1,500 visitors a day ascend Britain's most popular mountain by various routes at the height of the season.

A further 1,000 visitors a day reach the top by the 8-kilometre (5-mile) long rack-and-pinion railway that climbs almost to the summit. Although serious hill-walkers scorn it, it is an impressive feat of engineering, dating from 1896. Today, the 70-year-old steam locomotives (some carriages date back over 100 years) still make the summit in just under an hour – though nowadays there are also diesel locomotives and a diesel railcar unit. On especially clear days it is possible from the top to see the Wicklow Mountains in Ireland.

At the superb textbook cirque of Cwm Idwal is the first NNR to be established in Wales. Towering above the lake that fills this ice-sculpted hollow are the gaunt, precipitous grey cliffs of Glyder Fawr.

They are riven by a dramatic jointed cleft, usually known by its English name of The Devil's Kitchen (because of the fine steam-like haze of water that runs down from the cliffs). The Welsh call it Twll Du (Black Hole). Here, safe from the relentlessly nibbling mouths of the sheep, a select group of arctic-alpine wildflowers, relics of the Ice Age, hang on to almost inaccessible wet rock ledges. They include Roseroot, Purple Saxifrage, Mountain Sorrel, Alpine Cinquefoil and Snowdon Lily, found nowhere else in Britain except Snowdonia.

Woodlands

The Park contains many lovely woodlands, including remnants of ancient Sessile Oak woodlands, and larger areas of Forestry Commission conifers (increasingly mixed with broadleaved trees). The oakwoods provide plenty to excite fern lovers, and rich insect populations. Breeding birds include summer-visiting Pied Flycatchers and Redstarts, and resident Chaffinches, various tits, Nuthatches and Treecreepers, Siskins and Redpolls. Sparrowhawks prey on the smaller birds.

Lakes, Streams and Waterfalls

With one of the highest rainfalls in Britain, the Park has some beautiful rivers and waterfalls, including the much-visited Swallow Falls at Betws-y-Coed, and many lakes, some popular, others – in the remoter mountain areas – rarely visited. They support breeding birds such as big, fish-eating Goosanders, Common Sandpipers, Dippers and Grey Wagtails.

Some lakes hold a localized species of fish – the Torgoch, a Welsh race of the Arctic Char, a northern member of the trout family. At the extreme eastern edge of the Park, Llyn Tegid (Lake Bala) – Wales's largest natural lake – is famous for another rare fish, the unique Gwyniad.

Snowdonia's Coast

Although much of the coastline lies outside the Park, it does include one especially beautiful stretch in the west, with three superb estuaries: the Dyfi, forming its southern border, the Mawddach and the Dwyryd. These hold a good range of seaside plants and a rich variety of breeding birds, as well as wintering species such as White-fronted Geese.

Above: *Ring Ouzels – the much rarer wilder, mountain relatives of the common Blackbird – are declining, partly due to disturbance by walkers.*

Overleaf: *The magnificent Nant Gwynant valley.*

NEWBOROUGH WARREN

One of Britain's Finest Dune Systems

A trip to Newborough Warren, on the south coast of the island of Anglesey (Ynys Môn), in north-west Wales, is worth it just for the stunning views across the water to the mainland with its magnificent backdrop of the mountains of Snowdonia and the Llŷn Peninsula. In addition this area has a superb NNR, protecting 633 hectares (1,565 acres) of varied habitats – mud and sand flats, saltmarsh, a large area of dunes, a freshwater lake, long sandy beaches, shingle ridges and low cliffs – with a rich assortment of wildlife.

Anglesey was once the major Welsh wheat-growing region, as the signs *Mam Cymru* ('The Mother of Wales') at the county border attest. In the 13th century it was a landscape of fertile farmland, and the town of Newborough was prosperous. However, this scene was to change radically during the early 14th century, when the area was inundated by vast quantities of sand, blown inland to blanket the fields and prevent crop-growing, gradually overwhelming farms and houses. Many

Top left: *A Raven croaks loudly as it comes in to land; Newborough Forest holds a great winter roost.*

Opposite, top: *Newborough Forest footpath.*

Opposite, bottom left: *Wild Pansies on the dunes at Newborough Warren.*

Opposite, bottom right: *Pintail winter in nationally important numbers in the Cefni Estuary.*

people had to move inland. The precise cause of this disaster is unknown, though it probably involved extreme climatic changes perhaps leading to prolonged severe storms, and to changes in land use.

Over succeeding centuries the situation grew steadily worse, until a law was enacted in 1561, during the reign of Queen Elizabeth I, to protect the Marram Grass growing on the dunes; the severe penalty for cutting the Marram Grass or destabilizing the evolving dunes in any way was death.

Over time the prevailing winds have created four main dune ridges, separated by damp hollows called 'dune slacks'. The name 'Warren' (as well as 'Burrows') was given to many places supporting large numbers of rabbits, introduced chiefly in the Middle Ages to provide meat, and at one time over 100,000 rabbits per year were trapped by warreners living here. Today there are far fewer rabbits, due to the deliberate spread of myxomatosis in the 1950s and the growth of the forestry plantation. Although the reduction in their grazing pressure can allow scrub to invade in places, it has benefited other plants such as orchids.

Newborough Forest

In 1948 the Forestry Commission began planting conifers, mainly Corsican Pines, on the dunes in the northern section of the Warren to stabilize the sand. This area of mature trees is known as Newborough Forest. Covering around 800 hectares (2,000 acres) and occupying about two-thirds of the total area of the Warren, it is the largest forest on Anglesey.

Although outside the NNR, it is an SSSI and contains some interesting woodland plants, including orchids. Insects include butterflies such as Small Heath, Common Blue and Dingy Skipper, and there are a few Red Squirrels. The forest also holds breeding Sparrowhawks, songbirds such as Goldcrests, tits, Redpolls, Siskins and sometimes Crossbills, as well as Woodcock in autumn and winter, and one of the largest winter roost sites of Ravens in Europe.

Malltraeth Pool

Immediately to the north of Newborough Forest lies the broad estuary of the River Cefni. At its head, a large area of saltmarsh fringes the eastern shore. Once the river continued to meander freely into the low-lying valley beyond, but in 1810 an embankment, the Cob, was built to exclude the sea, and the river was canalized to reclaim much of the surrounding marshes for agriculture. Luckily there are still many areas of wet meadowland, now

an SSSI. Ditches formed as the meanders of the river were cut off contain two rare water plants, Pillwort and Annual Starwort, as well as commoner Reed Canary-grass, Branched Bur-reed and Water Plantain.

Immediately behind the Cob lies Malltraeth Pool, which along with the Cefni Estuary is a superb site for birdwatchers. This, and many other parts of Anglesey, was immortalized by the great wildlife artist Charles Tunnicliffe, who lived at 'Shorelands', on the edge of the estuary at Malltraeth, from 1947 until his death in 1979. His house is now run as a bed-and-breakfast establishment. A selection of his superb paintings can be enjoyed at the Anglesey Heritage Gallery at Oriel Ynys Môn, just north of Llangefni, about 11 kilometres (7 miles) north east of Malltraeth.

In spring and autumn, migrants include an excellent range of waders, such as Spotted Redshanks and Black-tailed Godwits, while winter brings more waders, and wildfowl such as Pintail, and Bewick's and Whooper Swans from the Arctic.

Dune Flora

The dune system of Newborough Warren NNR is one of the largest and finest in the British Isles. Typical plant species of the mobile, seaward dunes are Sand Cat's-tail, Sea Spurge, Mouse-ear Chickweed and Wild Pansy, the latter providing food for caterpillars of Dark Green Fritillary butterflies. Further inland, where the dunes are more stable, you can find Wild Thyme, Meadow Saxifrage, Tormentil and Common Bird's-foot Trefoil.

In the dune slacks the moist conditions enable Buck's-horn Plantain, Butterwort, Grass of Parnassus

and Creeping Willow to grow, as well as a whole range of orchids. These include good numbers of Dune Helleborines.

Birds breeding among the dunes include Tree Pipits, Whinchats, Stonechats, Grasshopper Warblers, Whitethroats and Yellowhammers, as well as Shelduck, while winter brings Hen Harriers, Merlins, Short-eared Owls and occasionally Barn Owls.

Cormorant City

At the south-west tip of the reserve lies Ynys Llanddwyn (Llanddwyn Island) – a peninsula that only becomes an island at very high tides. A narrow ridge of ancient Pre-Cambrian rock, over 600 million years old, ends here after running through Newborough Forest. Llanddwyn means 'the church of Saint Dwynwen'; the Welsh patron saint of lovers, she lived here during the 5th century AD.

Llanddwyn was once an important port for the arrival of slate (used in Anglesey, as throughout Wales, for roofing) quarried in Snowdonia and shipped from the mainland ports of Bangor, Caernarfon and Felinhelli. The old cottages, built to house the pilots who guided ships across the Menai Straits, have been renovated, and one now houses a local wildlife exhibition.

Unusual animal inhabitants of Llanddwyn are the tough little soft-fleeced Soay Sheep, the most primitive breed in the British Isles. They were introduced to the island and other parts of the reserve to graze and so discourage the development of scrub.

This is also a very good site for watching birds offshore, especially in the sheltered waters of Llanddwyn Bay: from spring to autumn these

Left: *The Cormorant can be seen all year in the area, and breeds, along with its close relative the Shag, on the rocks of Ynys yr Adar, off Llanddwyn Island.*

include Common, Arctic, Little and rare Roseate Terns and Red-breasted Mergansers, while in winter you can look for divers, grebes and sea-ducks such as Goldeneye, Eider, Common Scoters and Long-tailed Duck.

Off the tip of Llanddwyn, the islet of Ynys yr Adar (Bird Rock) is thronged with the black reptilian-looking shapes of Cormorants and Shags in spring and early summer.

Below: *For much of the year, Newborough Warren NNR is a wonderfully quiet place to get away from it all, with the bonus of superb views of the mountains of Snowdonia as a backdrop.*

SCOTLAND

THE BRITISH ISLES' GRANDEST AND REMOTEST LANDSCAPES are found in the far north, in Scotland. Two-thirds of its 77,167 square kilometres (29,797 square miles) are mountain and moorland, with many fine lochs (lakes) and rivers.

North of the Highland Boundary Fault lies the sparsely populated Highlands, including areas of almost true wilderness. The southerly part, the Grampians, has the highest mountains in the British Isles – including the magnificent Cairngorms, and Ben Nevis, the highest peak – and remnants of ancient native pine forests, notably in the Spey valley. The

northernmost area, the North-West Highlands, contains some of Europe's finest seabird colonies, as well as other scarce breeding birds, such as divers.

Although only 442 kilometres (275 miles) long and less than 250 kilometres (155 miles) at its widest, mainland Scotland has nearly 4,000 kilometres (2,500 miles) of coast, due to the fiord-like sea lochs that cut deeply into the western coastline.

Scotland is blessed with many plants and animals that do not generally live or breed elsewhere in the British Isles, such as the Golden Eagle, Capercaillie, Scottish Wild Cat and Azure Hawker Dragonfly. Its first National Park will cover picturesque Loch Lomond and the Trossach mountains, less than 40 kilometres (25 miles) from the centre of Glasgow.

There are almost 800 offshore islands, of which about 125 are permanently populated. Off the west coast lie the Inner and Outer Hebrides (the latter frequently referred to as the Western Isles), while off the north-east coast are the island groups of Orkney and Shetland. All are unspoilt, wildlife-rich places for the traveller to truly 'get away from it all'.

Opposite, left: *Scotland holds about 90 percent of the breeding population of the Fulmar in Britain and Ireland.*

Below: *A view towards Inverpolly NNR showing Stac Pollaidh and Cul Beag.*

ST ABB'S HEAD

Seabirds, Wildflowers and Marine Life

Location: On the east coast of Scotland, about 64 km (40 miles) east of Edinburgh.

Climate: Relatively dry; warm, sunny summers and cold winters; usually windy, gales in autumn and winter.

When to Go: All year for walking and general natural history; April–July for nesting seabirds, wildflowers and butterflies; most bird migrants April–May and August–October; October–April for wintering wildfowl, seabirds and birds of prey.

Access: By road, from A1 onto A1107 at either Burnmouth (from north) or Cockburnspath (from south) to Coldingham, then B6438 to St Abbs; car park at the NNR at Northfield Farm, then via path to the head; alternatively via road to small car park by lighthouse. By rail, nearest station is Berwick-upon-Tweed, then taxi-bus to St Abbs.

Permits: None required.

Equipment: No special equipment required.

Facilities: Accommodation limited, including B&Bs in and around Eyemouth; more at Duns, about 19 km (12 miles) inland, and Berwick; several campsites, also youth hostel at Coldingham Bay. Visitor centre and café at the NNR. Paths lead east then north along cliff top to lighthouse area; guided walks in season. Divers can charter boats and equipment locally.

Watching Wildlife: Seabirds visible from cliff-top path, or boat trip; most wildflowers and butterflies on grassland above cliffs; superb marine life.

Visitor Activities: Birdwatching, botany, entomology, general natural history, walking, scuba diving, sea angling, surfing.

This superb rocky headland is situated about 21 kilometres (13 miles) north of the border between Scotland and England at the southern edge of the Firth of Forth, its rugged, wave-battered cliffs rising about 100 metres (330 feet) above the cold, grey-green waters of the North Sea. Many millions of years ago, powerful forces thrust the horizontal rock strata of the volcanic intrusion of Old Red Sandstone into dramatic folds. Wind and sea have eroded the rock into deep indentations and sea caves, as well as cutting off half-submerged rocks and offshore stacks.

St Abb's Head NNR, 78 hectares (192 acres) of cliffs and inland habitats, is managed jointly by the National Trust for Scotland and the Scottish Wildlife Trust. It extends from the remote fishing village of St Abbs north to Pettico Wick. The cliffs hold a very big, thriving seabird colony, and the area is noted for its wealth of migrant birds – both seabirds and landbirds – as well as a great variety of wildflowers. The sea here is one of the best diving sites in Europe, and is protected as the St Abbs and Eyemouth Voluntary Marine Reserve

Top left: *The colourful and distinctive Six-spot Burnet Moth is widespread throughout Britain.*

Opposite, above: *A view of the cliffs at St Abb's Head in summer shows massed ranks of Guillemots.*

Opposite, below left: *A Lightbulb Tunicate.*

Opposite, below right: *The Wolf-fish is a voracious feeder, with powerful jaws and sharp teeth.*

Fishing History

Little St Abbs, and the much larger fishing port of Eyemouth to the south, are among the few sheltered harbours along this part of the east coast of Scotland. They formed part of the chain of ports from the Shetlands to East Anglia that were home to a great herring fishery. Its history, including the great disaster of 1881 when many of the boats and the town's fishermen were swept away by a huge storm, is detailed at Eyemouth Museum. Although the vast herring shoals have long gone, trawlers still catch fish such as Turbot, Haddock and Cod, but the imminent collapse of stocks threatens what is left of a once-thriving fishing industry.

Wildflowers

More than 250 wildflower species have been recorded within the reserve. Grazing by sheep and cattle keeps the cliff-top grasses short and allows the flowers to thrive. Different soil types produce a diversity of plants, so species not normally found together can be seen in close proximity. Where the underlying rock is acid, there are plants such as Heath Milkwort and Tormentil, while on mineral-rich soils yellow Bird's-foot Trefoil and Yellow Rockrose contrast with purple expanses of heather.

In summer, the cliffs are adorned with pink Thrift, and white Sea Campion, while rare Scots Lovage – smaller than the garden herb – grows on the projecting finger of cliffs at White Heugh. Another cliff plant is Roseroot, a succulent yellow-flowered member of the stonecrop family named for the roselike fragrance of its cut roots. There are also

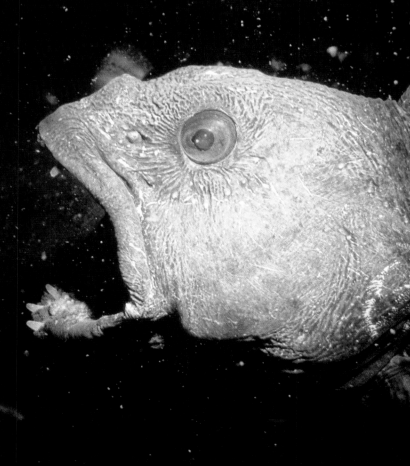

Above: *Kittiwake parent and chick; these attractive gulls breed in large numbers at St Abb's.*

great thickets of naturalized Japanese rose, a very thorny species introduced to Britain from Asia as a garden shrub and to enhance roadsides and deter burglars, covering the cliffs between St Abb's Head and Coldingham Bay.

It is not surprising that butterflies are abundant. These include Common Blue and Small Copper, as well as Grayling, Ringlet, the rare Northern Brown Argus and Dark Green Fritillary, and sometimes migrants, including Painted Lady and the occasional rare Camberwell Beauty. Moths include day-flying species such as the fast-flying Silver-Y and the boldly patterned Six-spot Burnet.

Seabird Cities

Some 60,000 seabirds breed annually. Most abundant, with some 16,000 pairs, are the noisy Kittiwakes that incessantly call their names, the rhythmic, nasal 'kitti-way-ake' producing an almost deafening chorus at close range. These elegant gulls incubate their eggs atop small, untidy flimsy-looking seaweed nests glued precariously to the tiniest of ledges high on the cliff face.

There are up to 13,000 pairs of dapper Guillemots, row after row perched on the long, winding, narrow ledges where they lay their eggs on the bare rock. Two other species of auks breed as well – several hundred pairs of Razorbills and about two dozen of Puffins. The great clefts in the cliffs allow for excellent views of the great throngs of birds. The densest populations are found on the stretch of cliffs below Headland Hill.

Other nesting seabirds include Herring and Lesser Black-backed Gulls, Fulmars, Cormorants and Shags; several pairs of Ravens breed on the higher ledges, and Rock Pipits build their nests in crevices in the rock below.

Seawatching

Its position makes St Abb's a great place for watching migrating seabirds offshore; Black Gable and the lighthouse are among the best (and most sheltered) places. Autumn is the best time, bringing many Manx Shearwaters and Great and Arctic Skuas, as well as smaller numbers of scarcer species such as Sooty Shearwaters, Pomarine Skuas and Little Gulls. Divers, grebes, Common Scoters and Eiders are regularly seen offshore in winter.

In summer, Guillemots and other auks may be seen whirring on their stubby wings to and from their breeding sites on fishing expeditions, dwarfed by gleaming white Gannets from the huge breeding colony at Bass Rock, situated about 39 kilometres (24 miles) to the north.

Other Migrants

Skylarks, Meadow Pipits, Stonechats and Wheatears breed on the headland, but many more landbirds pass through on migration in spring and autumn. East or south-easterly winds combined with rain, mist or drizzle bring the largest numbers of migrant birds. One of the best areas is around Mire Loch, a narrow artificial lake created in the valley behind the Head to attract migrant landbirds. These can include large numbers of thrushes, chats, flycatchers and warblers, and rarities, including Wrynecks, Red-breasted Flycatchers, Greenish, Arctic and Yellow-browed Warblers, Firecrests and Red-backed Shrikes. Winter brings Wigeon, Goldeneye and other ducks to the loch.

Marine Life

St Abb's Head is one of the few sites on the east coast of Britain with really clear water, and the strong tides ensure that the water remains free of pollution. These conditions allow the growth of submarine kelp forests, sheltering a great variety of marine life. The sheer rock faces, stacks and gullies are packed with colourful sea squirts, sea mats, hydroids and other animals, while in the beautiful, wild bay of Pettico Wick, the shingle seabed is littered with bigger rocks and boulders, providing hiding places for bottom-dwelling creatures such as brittle stars and delicate pink sea urchins.

A wide range of fish includes Lumpsuckers. In spring, they move inshore to the kelp beds. After mating, the females return to deeper waters, while the males guard the masses of pink eggs laid in depressions in the rocks. Above the water there is always a chance of seeing Grey Seals or Harbour Porpoises offshore.

CAIRNGORM & SPEYSIDE

Europe's Finest Mountain Reserve

The 1,000 square kilometres (400 square miles) of the great granite Cairngorm mountain range is the most extensive area of land over 900 metres (2,953 feet) high in the British Isles, and is destined to become one of Scotland's first National Parks. Britain's largest nature reserve, Cairngorm NNR, protects over 260 square kilometres (100 square miles) of this wild country. On the high mountain plateau, it includes the closest British habitat to that found in the Arctic as well as great expanses of moorland and bog. The region is bounded by clear rushing rivers, including the Spey, famed for its Salmon, and there are tumbling streams, sparkling lochs and ancient woodlands of native Scots Pine. The wide range of habitats ensures a great variety of wildlife, including species that are rare or absent from elsewhere in Britain.

The high plateau is dominated by great domelike summits, riven by glens (deep, narrow valleys), both created by huge glaciers during succeeding ice ages. Six of the summits are over 1,219 metres (4,000 feet) high, including Cairn Gorm itself, 1,245 metres (4,084 feet), and Ben Macdui, at 1,309 metres (4,295 feet) the second highest mountain in the British Isles after Ben Nevis (1,344 metres/4,409 feet), over 80 kilometres (50 miles) away to the west. This is the wildest part of these

Top right: *A Mountain Hare in its patchy spring coat is still camouflaged as the snow melts.*

islands, with spectacular scenery all year for the walker, climber, naturalist and angler. It is the site of Britain's most famous winter sports centre, based around the busy tourist resort of Aviemore.

Heather grows on the moors, giving way to a sparser cover of tough grasses, sedges and mosses. On the bleak high plateaux only lichens and mosses and a few very hardy plants survive, including Hare's-foot Sedge, Mat Grass, Three-leaved Rush and Moss Campion.

More snow falls here than on any other mountainous area in the British Isles. Some of the high corries have snow virtually all year round, and winds can reach 240 kilometres/hour (150 miles/hour). It is vital to have proper equipment, including a map and compass, and to take care – sunshine can give way to gales, driving rain or blizzards with alarming speed at any season.

Special Birds

The mountains have special birds: some – Peregrines, Red Grouse, Golden Plovers and Ravens – are widespread elsewhere, but others – Golden Eagles, Ptarmigans, Dotterels and Snow Buntings – are scarce Scottish specialities. Golden Eagles breed on remote crags and hunt Mountain Hares, Red Grouse and other prey, or search for carrion. The other three species live on the high tops, where there are few other signs of life.

Ptarmigans are high-mountain grouse, spending all year up on the tops unless driven lower down in

Location: The huge Cairngorm mountain plateau occupies the whole of north-east Highland Scotland between the Rivers Spey and Tay, overlooking Speyside in the north.

Climate: Relatively cool; summers can bring warm, sunny weather; winters can be very cold, with nearly arctic conditions on the high tops, and snow for much of the year.

When to Go: Any time of year for a great range of wildlife (apart from Ospreys – see below); superb walking and climbing.

Access: By road, via A9 for the south-western, western and northern sides of the Cairngorms and Speyside; A93 for central and south east; A939 for the north east. By rail, Kingussie and Aviemore stations between Perth and Inverness.

Permits: None required.

Equipment: Waterproofs and fleece are advisable.

Facilities: Plenty of accommodation, especially around Aviemore, booking essential in summer holiday and winter skiing periods; hotels and B&Bs, camp/caravan sites; youth hostels at Aviemore and Braemar.

Watching Wildlife: Britain's finest selection of mountain and ancient native pine forest wildlife is here, including Golden Eagles, Ptarmigan, Crested Tits and Mountain Hares, as well as Ospreys (centre at Loch Garten RSPB reserve open all day late April–August, once birds re-established following return from winter quarters in Africa).

Visitor Activities: Walking, climbing, skiing and winter sports, canoeing and watersports, riding, fishing, birdwatching, botany, general natural history.

Map labels

Grantown-on-Spey
Cromdale
Tomnavoulin
Auchnarrow
Avon
A95
A938
Carrbridge
A95
Spey
B970
Boat of Garten
Nethy Bridge
Abernethy Forest
RSPB Visitor Centre
Loch Garten Reserve
Aviemore
Glen More Forest Park
Monadhliath Mountains
Coylumbridge
A9
Cairngorm Ski Lift
Cairn Gorm
▲ 1245m
(4084ft)
A939
Corgarff
Kincraig
Rothiemurchus Forest
Feshiebridge
B970
Kingussie
Ben Macdui
▲ 1309m
(4295ft)
Newtonmore
Insh
Cairngorm NNR
Achlean
Cairngorm Mountains
Crathie
A93
Braemar
Glenfeshie Forest
Inverey
Gaick Forest
Grampian Mountains
N

Right: Small numbers of Snow Buntings breed on Cairngorm summits; during heavy snows they descend lower, and feed around car parks and chairlift stations.

Opposite, right: In northern Scotland the Stoat's fur often turns all white in winter, apart from the black tip to its tail.

Below: The high tops of the Cairngorms in winter. There are plans to make the Cairngorms a National Park.

particularly severe weather. They survive blizzards by tunnelling into snow drifts and roosting in the relative warmth of their shelters. Snow Buntings, too, occur here year round, with small numbers breeding and winter visitors being particularly easy to see around the ski lift stations and car parks.

From May to August, the Cairngorm plateau is the British stronghold for Dotterels, plump little plovers that are rare summer visitors, wintering in North Africa. Although they can be surprisingly tame, it is vital to avoid disturbing them and the other rare breeding birds.

Speyside Forests

After the last Ice Age, much of Scotland became covered by vast pine forests. For thousands of years, these ancient Caledonian forests flourished, growing up to about 600 metres (1,967 feet). However, from the 16th century much was cleared for farming and to provide timber for building, fuel and for industry, particularly during the two World Wars.

Today only about 80 square kilometres (31 square miles) remain, much of it in Speyside. Great swathes were replanted with conifers in uniform rows. By contrast, the ancient forest contains Scots Pines of all ages, some of them 300 years old. Open glades allow light to penetrate the dense, dark foliage, encouraging smaller Birch, Rowan, Aspen and Juniper, and a rich ground layer of plants and special wildflowers such as various species of wintergreens, Twinflower and Creeping Lady's

Tresses. There are also boggy areas with their own special plants and animals. This complex structure provides a great range of niches for a rich variety of insects, birds and other wildlife.

The RSPB reserve of Abernethy Forest, a mosaic of forest, mountain plateau and moorland, includes Loch Garten, famous as being the place where the Osprey first returned to Scotland to nest after ceasing to breed in 1916 as a result of persecution and the depredations of egg collectors. The first pair bred successfully in 1954, and nearly two million people have since come to watch pairs at their nest sites. The observatory at the visitor centre is equipped with binoculars, telescopes and a closed-circuit TV system.

For the thrilling spectacle of an Osprey diving down to seize a silvery Trout, visit Inverdruie Fish Farm on the outskirts of Aviemore. Another good place for seeing fishing Ospreys is Loch Morlich.

The Speyside forests also have Crested Tits, easy to recognize by their prominent spiky crests and distinctive trilling calls. The Scottish Crossbill, the only bird species restricted to the British Isles, is found only in the old Caledonian forests of north–central Scotland with mature Scots Pines.

Capercaillies, at the other end of the size scale, are huge, elusive grouse, best looked for very early

in the morning, when one might be seen whirring noisily out of a tree top. In spring, males gather at communal arenas, or leks, in forest glades. Here they compete by displaying to watching females, strutting with heads held high and tails fanned, and uttering a series of extraordinary sounds. Particularly aggressive individuals have been known to attack dogs and humans. Like the Black Grouse that live at the forest edge, Capercaillies are suffering a serious decline. As well as loss of suitable habitat, many are killed by crashing into 3-metre (10-foot) high deer fences, erected to protect young trees from being eaten by deer.

There are also plenty of Red Squirrels (in one of their chief British strongholds), Red and Roe Deer, the former in large herds, the latter in small family parties. Other mammals are largely nocturnal, and include Badgers, Foxes and rare Pine Martens, sometimes visible from hides or special feeding sites. Otters are found along the rivers and by the lochs. Wild Cats are particularly elusive; rare sightings are usually via car headlights or torches.

Left: *In a flurry of spray, an Osprey seizes a Trout after a dramatic dive and plunge into the water.*

Below: *A fine Red Deer stag prepares to challenge any rivals at Speyside during the rut in October.*

INVERPOLLY

Remote North-Western Wilderness

Location: In the Highland region of north-west Scotland, 19 km (12 miles) north of Ullapool.

Climate: Mild and wet, with relatively cool summers; winters can bring harsh weather, with much rain, mist and snow. Paths can be very muddy, and slippery in rocky parts.

When to Go: April–June best for birds, wildflowers and general natural history, although the scenery is also superb in autumn and winter. Biting midges can be a problem between April and October.

Access: By road, via A835 to Ullapool, and then continue on A835 to visitor centre at Knockan, 4 km (2½ miles) south west of Elphin. Summer bus service from Inverness via Ullapool to Durness passes reserve.

Permits: None required, but access to hills in Drumrunie area between 15 July and 21 October may be denied by Assynt estate office: contact warden.

Equipment: Waterproofs and fleece are advisable.

Facilities: Plenty of accommodation in Ullapool, including hotels and B&Bs, with self-catering accommodation and campsites in surrounding area. Information centre at Knockan, plus Knockan Cliff nature and geological trail.

Watching Wildlife: A wonderful place for birdwatching, with many Highland specialities breeding as well as a wide range of other birds. Wide range of wildflowers, ferns, liverworts, mosses and lichens.

Visitor Activities: Birdwatching, botany, entomology, general natural history, walking, climbing.

I nverpolly NNR is Britain's second largest nature reserve (after Cairngorm NNR: see pages 129–33), occupying 10,856 hectares (26,825 acres) of wild, rugged country in north-west Scotland. Most of its undulating plateau consists of a seemingly endless vista of rocky hummocks, interspersed with boggy hollows and dotted with many burns (small streams), lochans (small lochs) and lochs, including the extensive Loch Sionascaig, with its complex indented shoreline. There are also large lochs on the reserve's northern and southern boundaries. These include long, narrow Loch Veyatie in the north, and Loch Lurgainn in the south, where the reserve borders another large reserve, Ben More Coigach, which is managed by the Scottish Wildlife Trust. Along its north-western boundary, this outstanding reserve includes a beautiful stretch of coast and small islands.

With only three narrow roads skirting three sides of the reserve, and few tracks across it, this is one of the wildest nature reserves in the British Isles. Within minutes of leaving the road civilization is out of sight, and it is possible to roam all day without seeing another human being. The experience of being in such a remote place in these generally crowded islands, in good weather at least, is one that should not be missed.

Above, left: *Ptarmigan are one of the special birds found in the arctic-alpine habitats of the Highlands.*

Opposite: *One of Inverpolly's mountain streams.*

Great jagged red peaks of Torridonian sandstone tower over this huge expanse of wilderness. Cul Mor is the highest of these mountains, with one of its twin summits reaching 849 metres (2,785 feet), while Cul Beag is 769 metres (2,523 feet), but the most dramatic of all is Stac Pollaidh, with its summit at 613 metres (2,011 feet). The narrow ridge leading to the summit consists of shattered pinnacles of rock, eroded into fantastic shapes, looking like a strange fairytale castle or futuristic city.

A number of paths lead to the mountains, and climbs, though fairly strenuous, are generally straightforward and, in reasonable weather, guarantee superb panoramic views; however, only experienced climbers should tackle the summit of Stac Pollaidh, which is dangerous and crumbling.

Geological Importance

Inverpolly is one of Britain's most important geological sites, brought to a focus at Knockan Cliff, in the east, where the older rocks are not bedded beneath the younger ones as usual, but lie at the surface. In 1859, Professor Nicol interpreted this anomaly by arguing that the normal sequence of rock layers had become broken by a fault in the earth's crust, and the older rocks had been forced on top of the younger layers. Although most geologists of the time disputed Nicol's theory, it has since been recognized as an important and worldwide process.

The cliffs at Knockan are owned by Scottish Natural Heritage, but most of the reserve belongs to three private estates, and there are restrictions on access to some areas between July and October because of grouse shooting and deer stalking.

Plant Life

Over 360 plant species have been recorded. On the damp heathland are Heather, Cotton Grass, Purple Moorgrass and Deergrass. Bog Asphodel grows in the wetter areas, as well as Bog Myrtle. The lochans contain Intermediate Bladderwort and Bogbean, while Great Sundew, Lesser Bladderwort and two species of butterwort grow around their edges.

The many small patches of woodland are the remnants of once extensive prehistoric Birch and Hazel. Today, Birch is dominant, with Hazel, Holly, Rowan, Oak and Bird Cherry. In some places the soil is fertile enough for wildflowers, including Common Dog-violet, Meadowsweet, Melancholy Thistle and Selfheal. Ferns are often abundant, including Lemon-scented Fern, Wilson's Filmy-Fern and Hay-scented Buckler-Fern, and there are many liverworts, mosses and lichens.

Birds

Breeding birds include the relatively small Red-throated and the much scarcer Black-throated Diver. The former prefers to nest by the small lochans, flying to the sea to feed, while the latter favours larger lochs. Both are very vulnerable to disturbance, so it is vital not to approach nests during the breeding season, from May to August.

Other breeding waterbirds, especially by the coast, include truly wild Greylag Geese (rather than the feral ones found in many other parts of Britain), Wigeon, Red-breasted Mergansers and Goosanders. Along the coast and islands, Fulmars, Shags, Eider and Black Guillemots nest.

The moorland holds Golden Plovers and Greenshank, while there are Woodcock, Wood Warblers, Spotted Flycatchers and Treecreepers in the Birch woodland, where occasionally a few Redwings, best known as winter visitors to Britain from Iceland and Scandinavia, stay to breed.

On the high tops of the mountains, look out for Ptarmigans and Snow Buntings; at lower levels there are Red Grouse, and Ring Ouzels among the rocky gullies. The whole area is an excellent place for seeing Golden Eagles, though a pair range over a huge area when hunting. Don't confuse them with Buzzards, known to locals as 'tourists' eagles' – like eagles, they soar, but less majestically and in

Above: Mirrored in the waters of one of Inverpolly's lochs, the dramatic shape of Stac Pollaidh is a distinctive landmark, and a challenging climb for the experienced only.

There is a visitor centre beneath Knockan Cliff, with information about the geology and wildlife of the reserve, and a nature and geological trail. The trails climb up the cliff side to the crest, where there are ancient tree stumps embedded in the peat, 4,000-year-old remnants of the Caledonian pine forests that covered much of Scotland in prehistoric times. There are spectacular views at the top: this is a good way of checking for divers and other birds on the lochs, and there is always a chance of spotting a Golden Eagle.

Right: One of Inverpolly's most exciting mammals is the Wild Cat; very wary and most active at dawn and dusk, it is hard to see – look for the distinctive thick, bushy, blunt-ended tail with separate black rings, of which the end one is particularly broad.

closer circles. Unlike eagles, they often perch on roadside poles or posts, and sometimes hover; more often than not their loud mewing calls betray them. Other birds of prey include Peregrines and Merlins, and Ravens are a common sight.

Other Wildlife

Over 700 Red Deer roam over the reserve, and small groups are often seen. They are more obvious in winter; in summer they tend to move onto higher ground.

Badgers also occur in the reserve; unable to dig out their usual setts, since the ground is mainly bare rock, they make their dens in holes among the rocks. Two much rarer mammals are the Wild Cat and Pine Marten – like the others, they are mainly nocturnal, and very wary, though you may be lucky and see them at dawn or dusk

The lochs contain Trout, Salmon and Arctic Char, as well as Eels. These form the major prey of Otters, which are quite numerous, but elusive.

Top: *The Golden Eagle is an impressive predator, with a wingspan of up to 2.2 metres (over 7 feet).*

Right: *Otters thrive in the sparsely populated High-lands, including Inverpolly.*

THE HEBRIDES

Scotland's Western Island Chain

There are over 500 Hebridean islands, ranging from quite sizeable land masses to tiny islets, and stretching for 386 kilometres (240 miles) off Scotland's west coast. Divided into two major groups, the Inner and Outer Hebrides, they have been inhabited since prehistoric times. For the past 200 years most of the islanders have lived as crofters (smallholders), farming a few acres and sharing tasks such as peat-cutting, haymaking and sheep-shearing. 'Croft' comes from the Gaelic *croitean*, a small enclosed field.

The population is little more than 30,000, making this one of the most sparsely populated regions of Western Europe; fewer than 100 islands are inhabited. Most islanders earn their living from varied occupations: fishing, building and tourism, supplemented by crofting.

The Inner Hebrides

The large island of Islay (pronounced 'Eye-la') is the most southerly and one of the most beautiful and fertile islands, renowned for its superb single malt whiskies. The wildlife too is spectacular:

Top left: *Thanks to crofters practising traditional harvesting, the decline in Corncrake numbers is slowly beginning to reverse in the Western Isles.*

Opposite, top: *The Cuillin Mountains, Isle of Skye.*

Opposite, bottom: *The Old Village, Hirta, in the St Kilda archipelago, once home to a hardy community.*

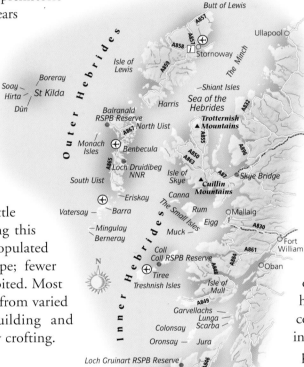

at sites such as the Loch Gruinart RSPB reserve over 40,000 Barnacle and White-fronted Geese visit in winter from their breeding grounds in Greenland, forming the greatest concentrations of wild geese in Britain. Other winter birds include Great Northern Divers and Whooper Swans; Golden Eagles, Hen Harriers, Peregrines and Barn Owls. Red-billed Choughs can be seen all year, as well as Otters, Brown Hares and Red Deer.

The Small Isles are Muck, Eigg, Rum and Canna. Rum (or Rhum), with huge sea cliffs and black volcanic mountains, shares with the Welsh island of Skomer the distinction of having the largest breeding colony of Manx Shearwaters in the world, over 100,000 pairs nesting uniquely near the mountain tops. The island has a large population of Red Deer, several pairs of breeding Golden Eagles, and is the site of a programme to reintroduce the White-tailed Eagle, which became extinct in Scotland in 1917.

Skye is the largest and northernmost of the Inner Hebrides, and has much of the grandeur of the Highlands, with the most dramatic mountains in the Hebrides. The mighty Red and Black Cuillin in the south (including Sgurr Alasdair, the highest peak at 993 metres/3,257 feet), and the jagged basalt pinnacles of Trotternish in the north are popular with tough walkers and rock-climbers.

NO. 8.
1930-EMPTY
FORMERLY CALLUM
MacDONALD.."OLD
BLIND CALLUM"

The Outer Hebrides

The great chain of the Outer Hebrides ('Western Isles' or 'The Long Isle') curves for 210 kilometres (130 miles) from the Butt of Lewis in the north to Barra Head in the south. Their east coasts are cut by long, narrow sea lochs, while the west has miles of lonely, unspoiled white beaches; in between lie heather-clad moorland and rugged hills.

The Outer Hebrides form a natural barrier protecting the Inner Hebridean islands and the north-west coast of Scotland from the Atlantic storms. Exposed to the full force of the sea, they experience dramatically rough, exhilarating weather in winter, while in summer can bask in sunshine.

Lewis is the largest island, and holds a good proportion of the total population. In the south the moors give way to hills towards the island of Harris, which is separated into two parts, mountainous North Harris and low-lying South Harris, by a very short and narrow isthmus at Tarbert. Some of the islanders are employed in weaving the woollen cloth known the world over as Harris Tweed, but the main focus of production has moved to Lewis.

The Machair

This very special habitat is the greatest wildlife glory of the Outer Hebrides. Lying behind the beach, and often including a zone of sand dunes, this flat plain of white, wind-blown sand is formed from countless crushed seashells, carpeted with grasses and a stunning display of wildflowers, intermixed with a mosaic of small lochs, crops and fallow land, often backed with marshy grazing land and moorland. In spring and summer there are Primroses, vetches, poppies, crane's-bills, orchids, Corn Marigolds and Harebells, with clouds of butterflies and other insects.

The most extensive areas lie in North and South Uist and Benbecula, with more local stretches in Harris and many of the smaller islands, including some in the Inner Hebrides. It is of huge importance for breeding waders, including internationally important numbers of Ringed Plovers and Dunlin,

Top, left: *Wildflowers adorn the machair grassland that is one of the Hebrides' crowning glories.*

Centre, left: *Gannets breed on the islands of St Kilda in greater numbers than anywhere else in the world.*

Bottom, left: *Soay sheep on Hirta, St Kilda.*

Opposite: *Kilt Rock Waterfall on Skye's east coast.*

as well as impressive concentrations of Oyster-catchers, Lapwings, Snipe and Redshank, and scarcer birds such as Little Terns and Corn Buntings. It is the last British stronghold of the Corncrake: this migratory relative of the common Coot and Moorhen returns from Africa in May, when males proclaim their territories and attract mates with their distinctive rasping two-note song.

There is increasing pressure on this unique landscape from agricultural developments, but traditional farming methods are being encouraged and research into the birds' breeding ecology goes on at RSPB reserves such as Balranald on South Uist and Coll in the Inner Hebrides.

Far-flung Outlier

Travellers with a sense of adventure will find it hard to resist a trip to St Kilda, lying in the Atlantic Ocean 160 kilometres (100 miles) west of mainland Scotland. One of the world's most spectacular wild places, it was designated Britain's first natural World Heritage Site in 1986, and is also a UNESCO Biosphere Reserve and NNR. Although there are cruises and charter vessels around the islands, the crossing (taking up to 48 hours if departing from Oban on the mainland) depends on the weather. The best way to see St Kilda is by paying to join the working parties carrying out restoration work on the ancient settlement at Village Bay on the main island, Hirta. These are run by the National Trust for Scotland, who lease St Kilda to Scottish Natural Heritage. Today, St Kilda's permanent human population consists only of a few British Army technicians, monitoring missiles fired from a base on Benbecula in the Outer Hebrides.

But for thousands of years St Kilda was home to one of the world's most isolated communities. They lived self-sufficiently, largely on seabirds and their eggs, obtained by scaling the terrifying cliffs using home-made horsehair ropes. After particularly stormy winters and increasing contact with the mainland, which brought disease as well as the lure of escape, the islanders eventually left their harsh but much-loved home for good in 1930.

This is the most incredible place. As the boat approaches the islands, huge sea stacks loom into view, white with a blizzard of countless Gannets. Connachair, the highest sheer sea cliff in the British Isles, towers 426 metres (1,398 feet) above the waves. The islands hold the largest gannetry in the world with 60,000 pairs, Britain's first and largest colony of Fulmars, and by far the largest Puffin colony, with an estimated 100,000 pairs.

THE NORTHERN ISLES: ORKNEY

Green Islands Thronged with Seabirds

Location: A group of islands, the most southerly 9.7 km (6 miles) north of the northernmost point on the Scottish mainland.

Climate: Often rainy or misty, and often with biting winds; summers are never hot, but can be gloriously sunny.

When to Go: Summer for breeding seabirds, wildflowers and almost constant daylight, but special rewards all year round.

Access: P&O ferries from Scrabster, near Thurso on the Scottish mainland, to Stromness, on the chief island of Mainland, and from there to the other islands; also British Airways flights from Aberdeen, Glasgow and Inverness to Kirkwall airport, on Mainland, with connecting flights from London, Birmingham and Manchester; also Loganair flights from Kirkwall serve some other islands.

Permits: None required, but warden should be contacted before visiting some reserves.

Equipment: Waterproofs and fleece are advisable.

Facilities: Most accommodation on Mainland, including hotels, B&Bs, self-catering accommodation, basic 'bothies', campsites and youth hostels.

Watching Wildlife: Shares with Shetland some of the world's finest seabird colonies, as well as other birds and the best selection of marine mammals, with various species of cetaceans viewable; also superb for wildflowers and marine life.

Visitor Activities: Birdwatching, botany, marine biology, general natural history, walking, archaeology (a great wealth of prehistoric sites, giving Orkney its title 'Egypt of the North'), fishing, sailing, diving.

Two major groups of islands, Orkney and more northerly Shetland, lie off the northwest of Scotland, where the North Sea meets the Atlantic. Colonized by the Vikings in the 9th century, they were ruled by the Norse earls until 1472, when they were annexed by Scotland. Unlike the people of the Scottish Highlands and Hebrides, the islanders have never spoken Gaelic, and their Viking heritage is reflected today in their architecture, customs and their singsong dialects (which include Old Norse words intermingled with a Scots-English base). They regard Scotland – let alone England – as a separate country, 'doon sooth' ('down south'), and restrict the term 'mainland' to the largest islands of each group.

It is possible to travel to and within both island groups by air, but using the frequent ferry services has the advantage that there is wildlife *en route*. Gannets plummeting beneath the waves for fish, whirring groups of Puffins, Guillemots and Razorbills, Common and Grey Seals, and many cetaceans – Harbour Porpoises are the commonest, but Minke, Long-finned Pilot and Killer Whales, and White-beaked and Risso's Dolphins are often sighted.

Land animals are mainly introduced. The Orkney Vole (a race of the European Common Vole) is preyed on by Hen Harriers and Short-eared Owls, and may have arrived as long ago as the Stone Age.

Northern Outposts

Despite the fact that these islands lie nearer to the Arctic Circle than to London, the climate is relatively mild, thanks to the warming influence of the Gulf Stream. But the weather can be among the most dramatic in Britain, with tremendous storms in winter. The wind blows almost constantly, and rain is frequent, though the weather is very variable, and summer can bring long spells of bright sunshine.

During the short winter days, outdoor pursuits are more limited, but there is still plenty of interest, with huge numbers of wintering waders, wildfowl and other birds, superb star-studded night skies free from light pollution, and stunning displays of the aurora borealis (northern lights) in September and October. A host of welcoming pubs awaits, with a wonderful, thriving tradition of folk music, especially fiddle-playing.

Top left: *Delicate and aptly-named European Jewel Anemones are found in Orkney waters.*

Opposite, top left: *The Arctic Skua nests in scattered colonies on moorland in Orkney.*

Opposite, centre left: *The Puffin breeds on the sea cliffs of many of Orkney's islands.*

Opposite, bottom left: *Spring Squill is just one of many beautiful wildflowers to be enjoyed in Orkney.*

Opposite, right: *The great seabird breeding colonies at Marwick Head RSPB Reserve on the island of Mainland, Orkney.*

Above: *The Dahlia Anemone is the largest anemone found on British shores. It is normally found in deep water where it can grow to the size of a small plate.*

Below: *A diver swims close to the* Brummer. *This is one of Scapa Flow's most impressive wrecks.*

A Distinct Character

Orkney comprises some 70 islands (19 inhabited), occupying a total land area of 1,014 square kilometres (391 square miles). It lies just 9.7 kilometres (6 miles) across the Pentland Firth, where the tidal races are among the strongest in the world. There are 1,448 kilometres (900 miles) of coastline, with deserted white shell-sand beaches washed by azure seas, especially in the islands north of Mainland.

Apart from their common early history – and the fact that they both are among the best places in the world for watching seabirds and other wildlife – Orkney is very different from Shetland. Due to the rise in sea level following the melting of the ice after the last Ice Age, Orkney resembles the scattered pieces of a jigsaw. If the sea level fell again by 37 metres (120 feet), the islands would be reunited as one land mass. The islands are mainly low and gently rolling, and as well as sandy beaches there are rocky shores and sea cliffs, made mainly of Old Red Sandstone. Orcadians have been described as 'farmers with boats' and much of the land is fertile, its rich pastures supporting many beef cattle. The green fields are brilliant with countless wildflowers in spring and early summer. As in Shetland, this is open country, with only a few trees and shrubs apart from a few small plantations and those in towns and gardens.

Orkney has the greatest wealth of prehistoric archaeological sites in Europe, including huge Neolithic burial mounds, such as Maes Howe (2900BC) and settlements as at Skara Brae, standing stone circles and henges, and Iron Age brochs (circular fortified towers). By contrast, Burgar Hill is the site of the world's most productive wind generator, capable of supplying 20 per cent of the islands' energy needs.

Scapa Flow is one of the largest and best protected natural harbours in the world, and played a vital role as a British naval base in the two World Wars. The site of the scuttling of the defeated German Imperial fleet in June 1919, it is now one of Europe's prime diving sites, with wrecks of three huge battleships and four light cruisers.

In contrast to most of the islands, the southern island of Hoy (from the Norse 'High Island') has rugged moorland, and twin peaks rising to almost 500m (1,640 feet) in the north, beyond which a great wall of red sandstone sea cliffs rises vertically to 348 metres (1,142 feet) at St John's Head. Facing them is the Old Man of Hoy, Britain's tallest rock stack at 140 metres (459 feet). The stack consists of 137 metres (449 feet) of weathered sandstone, protected by a resistant basalt base. It was first scaled in 1966 by a three-man team led by the famous mountaineer Chris Bonnington.

Orkney has a number of excellent nature reserves, protecting the best remaining areas of heather moorland, boggy areas and lochans, as well as seabird-breeding colonies. At the large RSPB reserve of Birsay and Cottasgarth Moor there are important populations of breeding Hen Harriers and Short-eared Owls on the moorland, and nesting Red-throated Divers, Red-breasted Mergansers, Wigeon and Teal by the lochans.

Noup Cliffs RSPB reserve on Westray is the site of one of Britain's most impressive seabird cliffs, where almost 45,000 Guillemots and 13,000 pairs of Kittiwakes jostle for space. On the neighbouring island of Papa Westray (known to locals as Papay), North Hill RSPB reserve also has outstanding seabird colonies. This tiny island was one of the last refuges for that giant relative of the Guillemot, the extinct Great Auk, and has the world's shortest scheduled air service – just 100 seconds flying time from Westray. It also contains what is claimed to be the most ancient domestic building in Europe, the Neolithic Knap of Howar, some 5,000 years old.

On both these islands, the largest remaining area of endangered maritime heath in Britain supports major colonies of Arctic Terns, constantly on guard for Arctic Skuas that also breed and live by robbing the terns and other seabirds of fish. There are over

50 species of wildflowers, including the tiny pink-flowered Scottish Primrose, one of Britain's few endemic wildflowers, found only in a few places on the north coast of mainland Scotland and Orkney.

Above: *The spectacular sandstone sea stack of the Old Man of Hoy, off the island of Hoy, Orkney.*

Below: *The Ring of Brodgar, Mainland, is just one of Orkney's many spectacular prehistoric remains.*

THE NORTHERN ISLES: SHETLAND

Distant Outposts

The 100 or so islands making up Shetland, only 15 of which are continuously inhabited, occupy a total land area of 1,452 square kilometres (560 square miles). This is the most northerly part of Britain, lying about 96 kilometres (60 miles) north of Orkney, halfway to Norway.

The Shetland islands are much bleaker and hillier than Orkney and, apart from small patches of farmland spotted with hardy sheep and little Shetland ponies, are largely covered by grass and heather moorland and peat bogs dotted with small lochs (lochans). Most of the underlying rocks, including gneiss, schist and extremely hard granite, are similar to those of the Scottish Highlands, with the softer, newer Old Red Sandstone found in Orkney only in the west.

The coasts are fringed by dramatic sea cliffs, deeply indented by long, winding inlets ('voes') and eroded by the powerful seas to form jagged stacks, arches, caves and deep fissures. Nowhere in Shetland is more than 4.8

Top left: *Edmonton's Chickweed or Mouse-ear, growing among serpentine rock on Keen of Hamar NNR.*

Opposite, top: *Muckle Flugga lighthouse; beyond it is Out Stack, Britain's most northerly point.*

Opposite, bottom: *Blanket bog at Unst-Hermaness NNR, on the headland ending in Out Stack.*

kilometres (3 miles) from the sea. Crofting, strongly supplemented by fishing, was the traditional occupation of Shetlanders for centuries.

Since the late 1970s, the exploitation of huge reserves of oil and natural gas in the North Sea has had a major impact on the economy of Shetland, but has also brought with it the threat of accidents. This was realized on 5 January 1993, when the oil tanker *Braer* ran onto rocks in the south of Mainland Shetland. Although it released twice the quantity of oil spilled during the notorious *Exxon Valdez* disaster in Alaska, the damage was less serious than it could have been since the oil slick was broken up and eventually cleansed by the hurricane-force winds.

Superb Wildlife

The islands' northerly position – only 6 degrees south of the Arctic Circle – brings almost 19 hours of daylight each day for about six weeks in the height of summer. The twilight that replaces the darkness of night ('simmer dim'), resembles a very long and beautiful sunset, when it is possible to watch birds, read a book, or play golf on the most northerly course in Britain (on Whalsay), at midnight.

There is no better place in Europe to see Otters, which spend most of their time searching for food – or playing – on the seashore. Apart from these, as with Orkney (where Otters are much shyer) the most spectacular mammals are out at sea: whales,

Right: *The Great Skua breeds on wet grassy or heathery moorland, often on the tops of high sea cliffs.*

Opposite, bottom: *Unst-Hermaness NNR has huge colonies of breeding seabirds, including these Puffins, amid some of the world's most superb sea-cliff scenery.*

Below: *The 180-metre (590-foot) cliffs on the island of Noss are home to one of Europe's finest seabird colonies, best seen from a summer boat trip that can be made around the island from Lerwick.*

dolphins, porpoises and seals. There are also many superb seabird colonies.

On Mainland, one of the best sites for watching breeding and migrating seabirds is Sumburgh Head RSPB reserve, in the south. There are breeding Guillemots, Puffins, Fulmars and Shags, while migrants include Sooty Shearwaters and Pomarine Skuas. A short distance north-west another RSPB reserve, Loch of Spiggie, attracts up to 300 Whooper Swans, Greylag Geese, Wigeon and Goldeneye, mainly in autumn, and Long-tailed Duck in spring.

One of the most spectacular seabird colonies, which contains approximately 65,000 pairs of Guillemots, 7,000 pairs of Gannets and 10,000 pairs of Kittiwakes, occupies the cliffs on the little uninhabited island of Noss (NNR). There are also many pairs of Great Skuas breeding on the moorland: the biggest of their family, they live not only by pirating fish from other seabirds but also by killing many of them; they feed on discarded fish from trawlers and carrion too. The species' stronghold is in Shetland (with the largest colonies on Foula, 22.5 kilometres/14 miles west of Mainland), where it is known as the 'Bonxie'. These birds will dive-bomb anybody near their breeding colonies.

Fetlar is a superb RSPB reserve, where over 90 per cent of Britain's Red-necked Phalaropes breed by shallow pools. These dainty little waders, otherwise mainly restricted to the Arctic, with Shetland as a southern outpost, have an unusual feeding method: they swim rapidly round in circles, disturbing tiny invertebrates, which they then pick off the water surface with their needle-thin bills. The females take the lead in courtship and leave the male to incubate the eggs and care for the young alone while they find another mate. Shetland also holds over 90 per cent of the British breeding population of the Whimbrel, the smaller, stripe-headed cousin of the Curlew, which also breeds on the reserve, along with Lapwing, Golden Plover and Dunlin. Fetlar is also the only British breeding site of Snowy Owls. Rare visitors from the Arctic, a pair bred between 1967 and 1975; since then, odd individuals have appeared, mainly on neighbouring islands.

Unst-Hermaness NNR, a northern headland on the northernmost island of Unst, is the site of another huge mixed seabird colony, including about 25,000 pairs of Puffins. A most unusual visitor from 1972 to 1987, and 1990 to 1995, mainly in spring, has been a solitary Black-browed Albatross. Presumed to be the same

bird, it was nicknamed Albert (Ross). A world away from its original home – and any chance of a mate – in the southern hemisphere, it even built a nest among the Gannets in some years. Offshore, Out Stack is the most northerly point in Britain.

Fair Isle

The southernmost island, Fair Isle (its name comes from the Old Norse *faar*, meaning 'sheep') is isolated almost midway between the other Shetland islands and Orkney. With an area of only 11.6 square kilometres (4½ square miles), it is famed as a major resting place for huge numbers of migrant birds, including rarities, thanks to its position at the crossroads of numerous migration routes between Scandinavia, Iceland, Britain and further afield: almost 350 species have been recorded. It is the site of one of the world's most important bird observatories, established in 1948, and since 1954 has been in the care of the National Trust for Scotland.

As well as many spectacular 'falls' of common species, Fair Isle attracts rare birds from half the world, such as Pechora Pipits from the Arctic, Thrush Nightingales from Eastern Europe, Paddyfield Warblers from Asia and Short-toed Larks from Southern Europe. The best time for finding rarities is mid-September to mid-October, though spring also brings exciting birds.

A mosaic of green fields and wild heather-clad moorland, this is the most isolated continuously inhabited island in Britain. The permanent population of fewer than 100 people earn their living partly from fishing and the production of the famous Fair Isle pullovers and other knitted goods. Fair Isle has a spectacular rocky coastline with cliffs towering 198 metres (650 feet) above the waves, where 18 different species of seabirds breed.

Above: *The famous Shetland ponies roam free over the islands; they are so small that they are measured in inches rather than hands; the average height is 100 centimetres (39 inches).*

IRELAND

THE 84,421-SQUARE-KILOMETRE (32,597-square-mile) island of Ireland lies west of Great Britain across the Irish Sea. Four-fifths are within the Irish Republic, while the remaining one-fifth forms Northern Ireland, part of the United Kingdom.

The Gulf Stream helps to produce a mild, wet climate, encouraging a lush growth of plants – the island is sometimes called 'The Emerald Isle'– with a particularly fine fern flora. It also attracts huge numbers of wintering birds from Britain and Europe.

Prehistoric Ireland was probably almost completely wooded, but climate change and

clearance took their toll; today it is one of the least wooded parts of Europe. Some old oak-woods do remain, such as those protected in two National Parks, Killarney and Wicklow.

Other habitats include beautiful hill and mountain ranges, and the plant-rich limestone landscape of the Burren. There are extensive peat bogs (Ireland has the third greatest proportion of peat bog to land area, after Canada and Finland), slow-flowing rivers with broad estuaries, flood meadows, known as callows, attracting wildfowl and waders, and lakes, such as Lough Neagh and Strangford Lough, fascinating for the naturalist and holding large numbers of wintering wildfowl.

Because Ireland separated from the British Isles relatively early on, many animals and plants found in Britain do not occur there. On the other hand, Ireland's position on the extreme fringe of Europe makes the western coasts and headlands attractive to migratory birds, including rare wanderers from America. On many of its wonderful coasts and off-shore islands there are major colonies of breeding seabirds.

Opposite, left: *The stunning bright blue Spring Gentian flowers from April to June.*

Below: *The region known as the Burren, in western Ireland, is one of Europe's premier natural history sites, with a unique assemblage of plants growing on its extraordinary landscape of dry weathered limestone.*

KILLARNEY NATIONAL PARK

Ireland's Finest Native Woodlands

Location: Extending to the west and south of Killarney, Co Kerry, Irish Republic.

Climate: Very mild and wet, with cool summers and mild winters: it rains, on average, 200 days per year, though not usually heavily; spring and summer also bring glorious weather. Cooler and windier on the mountains; snow rarely lasts for long.

When to Go: Early summer or early autumn are the best times to avoid crowds while ensuring there are places open to stay or eat; also best for wildlife and scenery.

Access: From Killarney, via two pedestrian entrances immediately opposite St Mary's Cathedral, at the western end of New Street. Other access points for drivers, too, between Killarney and Galway Bridge off the N71 main Killarney–Cork road.

Permits: None required.

Equipment: Waterproofs are advisable.

Facilities: There are thousands of places to stay in Killarney and district, from campsites to 5-star hotels. In high summer, many are fully booked; in winter many are closed. Marked nature trails and the Kerry Way, Ireland's oldest long-distance footpath; variety of guided tours, including boat trips on the lakes.

Watching Wildlife: Fine trees, special shrubs and wildflowers, and has a very rich flora of ferns, mosses and liverworts, native Red Deer and other mammals, and unusual fish, insects and invertebrates; good for birds, especially in summer.

Visitor Activities: Walking, climbing, cycling, boat trips, angling, birdwatching, botany and other natural history, geology.

Killarney National Park, Ireland's first, was established in 1932 when Senator Arthur Vincent and his parents-in-law presented the Muckross Estate to the nation in memory of the Senator's late wife. The State gave little financial assistance to 'the Bourn–Vincent Memorial Park', which was run chiefly as a working farm open to the public, but Ireland's developing economy enabled the purchase of more land from the former Kenmare Estate. The Park's importance for nature conservation was recognized when it was designated a UNESCO Biosphere Reserve in 1981.

Although Killarney town – a good base for exploration – and the surrounding countryside are among the country's most popular holiday destinations, with over a million visitors each year, the Park's 10,236 hectares (25,293 acres) contain plenty of places to escape the crowds and enjoy the stunning scenery. Thanks to its complex geology, mild climate, and varied landscapes with a wide range of altitude, there is a great variety of wildlife. There is also a good system of roads, tracks and nature trails.

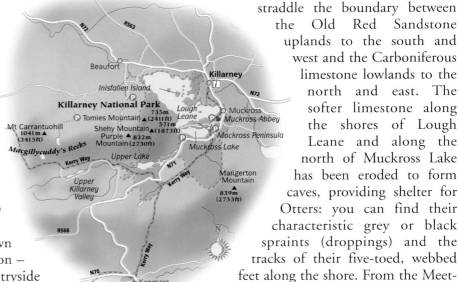

A Trio of Lakes

The Three Lakes of Killarney occupy nearly a quarter of the Park: Lough Leane (The Lower Lake); Muckross Lake (The Middle Lake); and the smallest, The Upper Lake, joined at The Meeting of the

Top left: *Within the British Isles, the Large-flowered Butterwort is unique to south-west Ireland.*

Opposite: *Torc Waterfall, Killarney National Park.*

Waters, a favourite beauty spot. Lough Leane is the largest at about 1,900 hectares (4,700 acres), while Muckross is the deepest near where the sheer face of Torc Mountain plunges 75 metres (250 feet) beneath the surface.

Lough Leane and Muckross Lake straddle the boundary between the Old Red Sandstone uplands to the south and west and the Carboniferous limestone lowlands to the north and east. The softer limestone along the shores of Lough Leane and along the north of Muckross Lake has been eroded to form caves, providing shelter for Otters: you can find their characteristic grey or black spraints (droppings) and the tracks of their five-toed, webbed feet along the shore. From the Meeting of the Waters, a narrow channel (The Long Range) leads to the spectacularly located Upper Lake, surrounded by rugged mountains.

There are many Brown Trout, and a run of Salmon upriver into the lakes in autumn. There are also two specialities. The Arctic Char, a relative of the trout, is a relict of the Ice Age; the Goureen or Killarney Shad, a member of the herring family, is a similarly landlocked endangered race unique to the Three Lakes.

A good range of wildfowl and ducks can be seen, especially in winter, including Teal, Pochard and Goldeneye, and Whooper Swans from Iceland.

Ancient Woodlands

On the lower slopes of Shehy and Tomies Mountains above Lough Leane lies the greatest remnant of the ancient oakwoods that once covered much of Ireland, occupying 1,200 hectares (3,000 acres) in the Park. The dominant trees are Sessile Oaks,

which thrive on the acid soil, above an understorey of shrubs, mainly Holly but including Hazel, Rowan and Downy Birch, and some supporting Ivy or Honeysuckle. The shady woodland floor is often covered with a great jumble of boulders. Few wildflowers grow there, but the star-shaped Yellow Celandines are beautiful in spring.

In more open areas (at the edge of the oakwoods and on clifftops) the evergreen Strawberry Tree can be found. Related to heathers, it bears rough scarlet fruits that are edible but sour (the specific name of the tree, *unedo*, means 'I eat only one'!) and are usually eaten only as jam. This frost-sensitive tree is a species characteristic of the Atlantic coasts of the Mediterranean. Another such plant is St Patrick's Cabbage (in fact a saxifrage); its cultivated form, London Pride, is well known to gardeners.

The Killarney oakwoods are noted for the rich growths of ferns, mosses and liverworts, many growing as epiphytes on the branches and trunks of the trees. Most special of all is the Killarney Fern, probably the rarest of the Park's many plants. Although relatively common during the 19th century, it suffered from the Victorians' craze for fern collecting and was picked almost to extinction. A member of the filmy fern family, it can be seen in a few isolated mountain sites where water splashes and there is plenty of humidity.

Reenadinna Wood lies on the Muckross Peninsula between Lough Leane and Muckross Lake, believed to be one of only three pure Yew woods in Europe. The ancient gnarled trunks emerge from a limestone pavement consisting of great blocks of angled stone resembling waves – indeed, they are known as reefs. The dense shade cast by the evergreen foliage prevents many flowers from growing, but mosses and liverworts flourish in the cool, damp microclimate: some areas are coated with blankets of moss which in places lies up to 15 centimetres (6 inches) deep.

One unwelcome inhabitant is the Rhododendron. Although a native of Ireland in prehistory, it was wiped out by climate change thousands of years ago. Reintroduced from the Black Sea region in the early 19th century, it now poses the biggest threat to the Park's woodlands; the rampant spread of its dense thickets cut out so much light that few plants can survive beneath it.

Woodland birds include Wrens, Robins, Goldcrests, Coal Tits, Treecreepers, Chaffinches, Siskins and Jays. Mammals include Wood Mice and Bank Voles (with unusually dense populations in the yew wood), Red Squirrels, Badgers and the highly elusive Pine Marten.

The Killarney woods and remote mountain slopes are also home to the only remaining herd of native Red Deer in Ireland, numbering some 700

Below: *A Killarney speciality is the Kerry Slug, which is protected under Irish law. As well as this dark type with whitish spots, there is a variety that is dark brown to bronze-olive with golden yellow spots.*

Far left: *Stunning scenery can be enjoyed from Lady's View, on the Ring of Kerry road, between Killarney and Kenmare.*

Left: *The Strawberry Tree, native to south-west Ireland but not to the rest of the British Isles, usually grows to 3–5 metres (10–16 feet) high, but some specimens at Killarney reach 10 metres (33 feet). Its very hard, fine-grained pink wood is highly valued by furniture makers.*

animals. Their close relatives, the Sika Deer, native to Japan and parts of the Far East, were introduced to the area in 1865. They thrived and now number about 2,000, preferring to stay in the woods, where they damage the trees by eating their bark; more seriously, they may start to interbreed with the Red Deer, threatening their genetic purity.

Woodland insects include Purple Hairstreak Butterflies, a great variety of moths, and over 30 species of gall wasps. One of the most remarkable animals to be found in the oakwoods is the Kerry Slug, a Lusitanian species that otherwise occurs only in Spain and Portugal. Often found on the sandstone boulders in the moorland as well, it can insinuate itself through tiny cracks by tripling the length of its body.

Mountain and Moorland

The mountains that form a rugged backdrop to the Park make fine walking country. The highest peaks are Mangerton (839 metres/2,753 feet) and Purple Mountain (832 metres/2,730 feet); the dramatic range of MacGillicuddy's Reeks, including Ireland's highest mountain, Carrantuohill (1,041 metres/3,415 feet) is visible from the Park.

Mountain birds include Hooded Crows, Ravens and Choughs; small numbers of Peregrine Falcons breed on isolated crags, while the Ring Ouzel is a scarce summer visitor.

Much of the higher ground is covered with blanket bog. Here, among the cotton grasses and other plants, grows the rare insectivorous Greater Butterwort, whose spectacular single purple flowers account for its popular misnomer 'Kerry Violet'. Good numbers of Snipe nest in the bogs, while a small flock of Greenland White-fronted Geese spend winter here.

Below: *A standing stone seen from the Ring of Kerry road; Killarney, as with many other parts of Ireland, has a rich heritage of ancient remains such as this.*

THE BURREN NATIONAL PARK

Rich Mixture of Plants in a Strange Landscape

Location: South of Galway Bay, in the north-west corner of Co Clare, Irish Republic, centred on Mullaghmore.

Climate: Mild and usually snow- and frost-free in winter, with lowest rainfall on west coast except on higher ground; can be very windy. Summer can bring glorious sunshine.

When to Go: Spring and early summer (late May to early June) for the greatest variety of wildflowers and butterflies.

Access: By car or bus via the N67 road through Kinvara and Bally-vaughan on the north coast. A great way to see the landscape is via the Burren Way from Lis-doonvarna to Ballyvaughan. The Burren NNR is at Slieve Carron. Catamaran tours from Liscannor in summer past Cliffs of Moher.

Permits: None necessary.

Equipment: No special equipment required.

Facilities: Doolin, Lisdoonvarna and Ballyvaughan have the greatest choice of accommodation, including camp and caravan sites, hostels and B&Bs, and of places to eat. The Burren Centre (open early March—end October) is in the village of Kilfenora. There is a year-round Visitor Centre at Cliffs of Moher.

Watching Wildlife: Renowned for its range of wildflowers concentrated in one area; also excellent for butterflies, moths and snails. The Cliffs of Moher are the highest sheer cliffs in mainland British Isles and have large colonies of Puffins and other breeding seabirds early May to end July, as well as Choughs.

Visitor Activities: Botany, bird-watching and wildlife-watching, geology, archaeology, religious history, walking, cycling, caving.

The extraordinary and sparsely populated area known as the Burren, occupying about 450 square kilometres (280 square miles) in the west of Ireland, is justly famed for its geological interest and exceptionally rich plant life.

About 340 and 300 million years ago, North-west Europe was periodically inundated by a warm, shallow sea. Huge beds of limestone formed from the shells and skeletons of countless marine invertebrates. Today, the limestone underlying much of Ireland is covered by shale and sandstone, built up from river-borne silt and sand, but in the Burren it became exposed by the scouring action of Ice Age glaciers and subsequent erosion by wind and rain.

About 25 per cent of its surface is bare limestone 'pavement', where weathering has split the smooth, fossil-rich expanses into a maze of slabs ('clints'), separated by deep fissures ('grykes'). In places frost has fragmented the rock, creating an almost lunar-style landscape, while elsewhere erosion has created dramatic, broad terraces. The moving ice left behind great boulders – erratics – often perched on a small pedestal of rock.

Top left: *Razorbills gather in scattered colonies on the massive cliffs of Moher. The rock-strewn sea cliffs provide suitable nesting sites.*

Opposite, left: *The splendid mixture of wildflowers found in the Burren includes Mountain Avens (top), Irish Saxifrage (centre) and Fly Orchid (bottom).*

Opposite, right: *The cliffs of Moher towering above the Atlantic waves.*

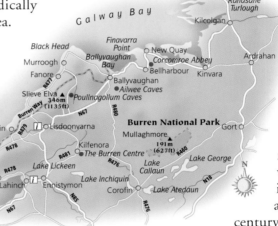

This remarkable landscape – the Burren is the largest continuous area in Western Europe – is known as karst, after a similar area in South-eastern Europe. Viewed from the coast the rounded, pale grey hills look like a great school of giant whales.

The area is rich in archaeological remains, with more than 400 earthen ring forts (raths), evidence of over 800 dwellings and 68 megalithic tombs, as well as beautifully inscribed Celtic crosses and the ruined 11th-century Cistercian abbey of Corcomroe. Ancient green roads crisscross the gaunt landscape, and there are abandoned villages dating from the great potato famine of the 1840s.

The attractive spa town (unique in Ireland) of Lisdoonvarna makes a fine base for exploring the area. Perhaps the best approach, though, is to start from the coast and explore the eastern part of the Burren, including the National Park, where the flowers are most spectacular.

Plant-hunter's Paradise

Although the Burren forms only 0.5 per cent of the total area of Ireland, it is home to 81 per cent of the 900 or so native plant species. The well-drained, lime-rich soil accumulated in the fissures supports a profusion of plants; there is also a mild, frost-free climate, abundant rain, and the bare rock traps warmth from the sun.

This great natural rock garden has an extraordinary mixture of wildflowers, best in early summer. A particularly good area is the 10-kilometre (6¼-mile) coastal strip between Poulsallagh and Black Head.

Mountain Avens, Spring Gentian and Bearberry, typical of high mountains and the Arctic, grow down to sea level beside Wild Madder and Maidenhair Fern, characteristic of the Mediterranean. There are Irish and Mossy Saxifrages, orchids, delicate Burnet Roses and Bloody Crane's-bill, whose purple blooms contrast dramatically with the pale grey rock.

Widespread hazel scrub provides welcome shelter for birds and mammals. The combined effects of the strong westerly winds and grazing frequently stunt the trunks and branches, which are clothed with lichens and mosses.

Limestone grassland is the dominant habitat in areas where the rock is overlain by a veneer of dark soil. Slender St.John's Wort, Wild Thyme and Fairy Flax grow among Blue Moor-Grass, while other areas are dominated by heather and large mosses.

Wildlife of the Burren

All but two of Ireland's 31 resident species of butterfly occur here (most of their caterpillars feed on limestone-loving plants) including the Pearl-bordered Fritillary, found nowhere else in Ireland. Moths include the rare day-flying Transparent Burnet Moth, and the Burren Green, otherwise found only on the European Continent.

Over 70 different species of snail have been found, from the tiny, delicate translucent *Vallonia excentrica*, to the Tree Snail, with its long spire-shaped shell. The commonest species is the Brown-lipped Banded Snail, with a bewildering range of colours and banding patterns. The snails' chief predator, the Song Thrush, concentrates on those that are less well camouflaged.

Mammals include Foxes, Badgers and Stoats, and that elusive and beautiful relative of the Stoat, the Pine Marten. Pygmy Shrews and Wood Mice are very common in the hazel scrub, while Otters occur and seals can be seen off the coast. Common Lizards – Ireland's only reptiles – sprawl on the rocks on sunny days.

The estuaries along the north coast provide rich feeding grounds for wildfowl, including Brent Geese and a good variety of waders. Peregrine Falcons breed on the cliffs, and Hen Harriers nest in young conifer plantations. The commonest open ground birds are Skylarks, Meadow Pipits, the latter attracting Cuckoos to lay in their nests, Stonechats and Wheatears, while 28 species, including Chiffchaffs, Bullfinches and Sparrow-hawks, have been recorded breeding in the scrub woodlands.

Below: *The naked limestone rocks of Mullaghmore loom above the flat landscape in this south-eastern corner of the Burren. At the mountain's foot are a series of small turloughs, seasonal lakes peculiar to limestone areas in western Ireland.*

On the Atlantic coast south-west of the Burren are the dark sandstone Cliffs of Moher (204 metres/670 feet). As well as providing nest sites for seabirds including Guillemots, Razorbills, Shags and the largest colony of Fulmars in Ireland, they have breeding Peregrines, Rock Doves (the wild ancestors of all town pigeons), Choughs, croaking Ravens and Twite, the northern relative of the Linnet.

Cave Systems

The Burren is famous for its spectacular caves, carved out by underground streams and rivers – all but one of its rivers, the Caher, are hidden. On the eastern flank of Slieve Elva, the highest peak (346 metres/1,135 feet), a chasm leads to the great Poullnagollum ('Cave of the Doves') cave system, the longest in Ireland at 15 kilometres (9⅓ miles).

Visitors can join a guided group to see the large Ailwee cave system, discovered in 1944 by a farmer searching for his sheepdog. The main passage is 600 metres (1,969 feet) long; there are waterfalls and impressive stalactites and stalagmites, and the remains of Brown Bears, extinct in the British Isles for thousands of years.

Disappearing Lakes

Known as turloughs, from the Irish for 'a dried-up place', these temporary lakes appear after heavy rain. They are connected to the subterranean water reservoir via 'swallow holes', up to 3 metres (10 feet) across, through which the water rises, often at an amazing speed. Usually water-filled in winter and empty in summer, they support a wealth of wildflowers, including great carpets of Fen Violets.

Rahasane Turlough, just outside the Burren in County Galway, is Ireland's largest, and attracts thousands of wildfowl and waders in winter, when over 275 hectares (680 acres) of flat grassland can be inundated with water.

Saving the Burren

Much of the south-eastern corner, around the great limestone terraces of Mullaghmore Mountain, is protected within the 1,673-hectare (4,134-acre) Burren National Park, established in 1991. Such protection is sorely needed; modern farming methods have had adverse effects on the natural habitats of the Burren. Many of the most flower-rich areas have been ruined by the application of fertilizers and herbicides, which encourage the growth of grasses at the expense of wildflowers.

Above: *The Poulnabrone Dolmen, one of Ireland's finest prehistoric monuments, is a burial chamber over 5,000 years old, with a huge capstone atop the tripod of supporting stones.*

WICKLOW MOUNTAINS NATIONAL PARK

A Historical Site and Impressive Scenery

Ireland's fourth National Park was established in 1991 with a core area of 3,697 hectares (9,135 acres) centred around the Glendalough valley and including the Glendalough Woods and Glenealo Valley NRs. The Park has since been greatly expanded, and today covers an area of almost 20,000 hectares (49,400 acres), protecting the internationally important Liffey Head and Lugnaquillia Bog areas. There are plans to enlarge it further to cover as much as 30,000 hectares (74,000 acres), extending the whole length of the Wicklow Mountains, to become Ireland's largest National Park.

Situated right on Dublin's doorstep, the Park can become very crowded, especially in summer; but it is always possible to find peace and tranquillity, and magnificent country for walking, climbing or wildlife-watching.

Monastic Settlement

The Glendalough valley was carved out by glaciers during the last Ice Age, and holds two lakes (Glendalough, Irish Gleann dá Loch, means 'Valley of the Two Lakes'). In AD 617 an early Christian

Top left: *The golden yellow flowers of Bog Asphodel brighten the bogs and wet moorland.*

Opposite, top: *The Wicklow Gap in summer.*

Opposite, bottom: *The Glendalough valley is one of Ireland's most famous beauty spots.*

bishop, St Kevin, founded a monastery on the southern shore of the Upper Lake, which was accessible only by boat. St Kevin was said to have lived in a small cave nearby.

Stories about him abound: that he chose this wild setting to escape from a beautiful amorous redhead with 'unholy eyes'; when she pursued him, he rolled around with her in a bed of nettles and flung her into the cold lake; that he visited Glendalough as a child and lived in a tree; or about how a bird trusted him so much she laid an egg in his hand! West of the Lower Lake is the Deer Stone: the legend is that when St Kevin had to feed two orphaned babies, a deer appeared and allowed herself to be milked.

This humble settlement eventually became a monastic city; in the Middle Ages seven pilgrimages to Glendalough were said to equal one to Rome. Vikings sacked the monastery at least four times from the 8th–11th centuries, and it was almost completely destroyed by English soldiers in 1398. It was rebuilt again, but the dissolution of the Irish monasteries in 1537 by King Henry VIII of England finally sealed its fate. Now a National Monument, most of what remains dates from the 8th–12th centuries, and includes a cathedral, several churches and a fine 33-metre (108-foot) 10th-century round tower.

Glendalough Woods

Large areas of semi-natural deciduous woodlands are protected around Glendalough; the biggest

Above: *Bluebells are among the host of beautiful wildflowers growing in the woods of Glendalough.*

Below: *The rare Alpine Lady's-Mantle grows on the rocky escarpment overlooking Lough Ouler; elsewhere in Ireland it occurs only at one site in Kerry.*

block lies on the flanks of Derrybawn Mountain. All are entirely secondary woodland, the original trees having been heavily coppiced or felled in the early 19th century, and are dominated by Sessile Oak, up to 15 metres (50 feet) in height, but generally smaller. Beeches are common, too, while conifers, especially Scots Pine and Larch, are widespread. The shrub layer includes Rowan, Hazel, Hawthorn, small Birch trees and Holly – as well as unwelcome patches of introduced Rhododendron. In spring Wood Anemones, Wood Sorrel and Bluebells beautify the woodland floor. Other common plants in the herb layer (rather sparse due to heavy grazing by sheep and deer) are Woodrush, Bilberry and a variety of grasses, ferns and mosses, while rarities include the Lemon-scented Fern and a particular species of clubmoss. Streams, lakes and rocks make for a diverse habitat for wildlife.

The woods provide nest sites for a variety of birds. The most abundant are Wrens, Robins, Goldcrests, Coal Tits and Chaffinches. Sparrowhawks, Blackcaps, Chiffchaffs and Jays are widespread, while Redstarts and Wood Warblers breed here in small numbers at one of their few Irish sites; a few pairs of Ring Ouzels nest among the boulders and scree on the mountain slopes above the woods. Grey Wagtails and Dippers grace the stream linking the Upper and Lower Lakes, which are sometimes visited by Whooper Swans in winter, and the elusive Grasshopper Warbler delivers its strange insect-like song – which also sounds like a fishing reel being wound – from cover by the Lower Lake.

Granite Mountains

The great spine of granite that forms the Wicklow Mountains is the largest upland area in Ireland (with 520 square kilometres/200 square miles over 300 metres/984 feet), and the largest exposed area of granite in the British Isles. Molten volcanic rock (magma) was forced up from deep underground some 400 millions of years ago, pushing aside the surrounding sedimentary rocks, then cooling to form immensely hard granite.

This molten rock transformed these sedimentary rocks into shiny mica schists, producing high concentrations of copper, iron, lead, silver and zinc. These valuable metals, especially lead, were mined on a large scale in the 19th century (involving up to 2,000 workers) and to a smaller extent from 1919 to 1950, at the western end of the Glendalough valley. Evidence today includes mine entrances, white spoil heaps, and planted Scots Pines (for pit props) on the northern shore of the Upper Lake, where Red Squirrels can be seen.

The Park includes the south-eastern slopes of Lugnaquillia, Wicklow's highest mountain at 925 metres (3,035 feet), and unusual in retaining its cap of Old Red Sandstone. Although the summit lies just outside the Park's boundary, there are several other high points within it: Tonelagee (816 metres/2,677 feet), Conavalla (734 metres/2,408 feet) and Djouce (727 metres/2,385 feet).

The great rounded mountains are covered by a mosaic of blanket bog, heather moorland and cliffs, scree slopes and rocky outcrops, with upland grassland in drier areas, with swathes of bracken and small pockets of woodland. Rare Parsley Fern, Bog Orchid and St Patrick's Cabbage grow here, the last far away from its main sites in Cork and Kerry. At Liffey Head scarce Bog Rosemary can be found, along with more abundant Bog Asphodel, Deergrass and cotton grasses. The corrie lakes, such as Lough Ouler and those at Lough Bray, are among the finest examples in eastern Ireland of these steep-sided crescent-shaped basins, carved out by Ice Age glaciers. Their deep, dark waters contain unusual plants, including Quillwort and Shoreweed, and arctic-alpine species of water boatmen and diving beetles, left behind when the glaciers retreated. At Raven's Glen, the shaded areas near the waterfall are home to many ferns, including Filmy Fern. The corrie cliffs at Lough Ouler soar to 100 metres (328 feet), and where the rock is schist it supports a rich alpine flora, including Golden Saxifrage, Starry Saxifrage and Dwarf Willow, and rare Alpine Lady's-Mantle.

Several birds of prey can be seen; the Kestrel is most abundant, but there is also a chance of seeing its dashing little relative the Merlin, while Peregrine Falcons breed on crags and cliffs, and there are several pairs of Hen Harriers. Snipe, Meadow Pipits, Skylarks, Ravens and Hooded Crows are widespread, while Red Grouse are sparsely distributed across the moorland. Crossbills are regular visitors to conifer plantations.

Foxes, Badgers and Mountain Hares are found on the moors, while wary Otters occur along the larger rivers. A small number of feral goats roam the slopes and cliffs, the males leaving behind their distinctive pungent smell. The most visible mammals are usually the Red Deer–Sika hybrids on the moors, crossbreeds between local Red Deer and introduced Sika Deer escapees from Viscount Powerscourt's estate.

Top, right: *A Wood Warbler at Wicklow, one of the few places in Ireland where it can be heard.*

Centre, right: *The tiny Goldcrest (Europe's smallest bird) is one of Ireland's commonest woodland birds.*

Bottom, right: *The mountains are home to a variety of flora including the delicate St. Patrick's Cabbage.*

THE GIANT'S CAUSEWAY & CAUSEWAY COAST

A Geological Phenomenon

The Giant's Causeway and Causeway Coast is not only a UK NNR, but also the only UNESCO World Heritage site in Northern Ireland, and has even been described as the eighth wonder of the world. The Causeway Coast is also an AONB, and the Causeway itself receives additional protection as an ASI and ASC.

Situated on the north Antrim coast, the outstanding feature here is a unique formation of massive, polygonal columns of rock emerging from the sea, arranged like giant stepping stones. In addition to the Giant's Causeway some other rock columns and formations bear evocative names, such as the Giant's Organ, Chimney Tops, the Honeycomb, the Wishing Well, the Giant's Granny and the King and his Nobles.

This remarkable place has attracted visitors for several hundred years: one of the first recorded visits was by the Bishop of Derry in 1692, although the Causeway did not come to general notice until the 18th-century Romantic Movement. Famous visitors included the novelists Sir Walter Scott and William Makepeace Thackeray. It became more accessible after the coast road was built in the 1830s; in 1883 the first hydroelectric tramway in the world was opened, and extended in 1887 to the Causeway Head. Today the site attracts over 350,000 visitors per year from all over the world.

Top left: *Early Purple Orchid, one of many clifftop flowers along the Causeway coast.*

Opposite: *The spectacular Giant's Causeway, one of Europe's premier geological sites.*

Famed in Folklore

It is hardly surprising that the columns inspired myths about their origin. In one legend Finn McCool or Fingal (in Gaelic Fionn McCumhaill), a legendary warrior, fell in love with a female giant who lived on the little Scottish island of Staffa in the southern Inner Hebrides. Finn built a great highway across the sea so that he could carry her back to Ireland.

In another version Benendonner, a Scots giant, built the causeway to reach Finn after the two had challenged each other to a fight. When Finn saw how big his rival was, he fled home and hid in the baby's crib. Benendonner strode into the house and was terrified: if this was the size of the baby, how big was its father? He rushed back to Scotland tearing up the bridge behind him, leaving only its ends: the Giant's Causeway, and a smaller area of basalt columns in Fingal's Cave on Staffa.

Remarkable Rocks

The columns consist of basalt, a fine-grained, dark, igneous rock, resulting from intense volcanic activity in the Tertiary Period 55 million years ago that formed the huge Antrim Plateau, the largest lava plateau in Europe. As the molten lava flowed into the sea it cooled rapidly, forming about 40,000 remarkable columns, averaging 45 centimetres (18 inches) across and 12 metres (40 feet) high. They are almost entirely regular in shape and most are hexagonal (six-sided).

The site has been of great international interest to geologists for some 300 years, and provided vital evidence in the 18th-century debate about the origins of basalt and other igneous rocks. It was

Above: *Crossing the spectacular Carrick-a-rede rope bridge, though not for those with any fear of heights, is a memorable experience. It was originally built to enable salmon fishermen to reach their huge fixed-engine fishing nets.*

Giant's Causeway have a stepped structure resulting from a succession of separate lava flows. From the clifftop path there are superb views over the sea, where Grey Seals can often be seen.

Near Port-na-Spaniagh is the site of the wrecked warship *Girona*, one of the ships in the first Spanish Armada that attempted to invade England in July 1588. After the Spanish fleet were routed off the French coast they fled north and many were lost due to a combination of battle damage and storms. The *Girona* took with her a crew of about 1,300 and a cargo of valuables, much of which was salvaged by the Belgian diver Robert Sténuit and his team between 1967 and 1969, and is displayed in the Ulster Museum in Belfast.

A recently constructed section of the path links Ballintoy harbour with Larrybane Head and Carrick-a-rede, with its famous 20-metre (65-foot) Rope Bridge across to a tiny island with an ancient Salmon fishery. The 24-metre (79-foot) high bridge, removed each winter, has handrails, but no more than two people should cross at once.

Varied Plantlife

Over 200 plant species have been recorded in the area. The clifftop vegetation includes maritime heath and grassland, with plants tolerant of sea spray and driving winds, such as Heath Spotted Orchid, Devil's-bit Scabious and scarce Sea Spleenwort, while Thrift and Bladder Campion decorate the slopes with pink and white flowers.

Many different lichens encrust the rocks, while at the base of the cliff grow Bluebells, Wood Stitchworts and Red and White Campions. Rare northern species such as Scots Lovage and Oysterplant find a home along the shore.

Birdlife

Fulmars, Guillemots, Razorbills and Puffins, Buzzards, Peregrines and Ravens nest on the cliffs. Golden Eagles are occasional; Benmore was their last breeding site in Northern Ireland (1953–60).

The short boat trip to Rathlin Island from Ballycastle is well worthwhile. Spectacular cliffs fringe the long east–west arm of this 1,400-hectare (3,460-acre) island, thronged with breeding seabirds in summer: 100,000 Guillemots and 21,000 Razorbills, one of the biggest colonies in the British Isles. There are eye-level views of the stacks from the West Lighthouse (leased by the RSPB, who have a reserve on the island). Other breeding seabirds include Shags, Fulmars, Puffins, Black Guillemots and Manx Shearwaters, while Eider Duck nest on the coasts of the southern arm. Landbirds include Rock Pipits and, sometimes, that wild-country relative of the Linnet, the Twite.

first recognized as the remains of a lava flow by the French geologist Nicolas Desmarest in 1771.

The Causeway Coast Path

Part of the 900-kilometre (559-mile) Ulster Way, the Causeway Coast Path runs along the cliffs for 22.5 kilometres (14 miles) from Blackfoot Strand, west of the Giant's Causeway, to Ballintoy harbour.

The 6-kilometre (3¾-mile) stretch of 100-metre (330-foot) basalt cliffs that stretch either side of the

Right: *A Black Guillemot in its striking breeding plumage; these seabirds breed in small numbers on Rathlin Island.*

STRANGFORD LOUGH

Northern Ireland's Premier Marine Site

This enormous sea lough, one of the largest in the British Isles, is of international importance for its impressive concentrations of wintering wildfowl and wading birds and for its marine life; it is Northern Ireland's first MNR, and the largest of the three statutory MNRs established in the UK to date.

Almost completely landlocked by the rich rolling farmland of County Down, it is separated in the east from the Irish Sea by the Ards Peninsula, and linked to it by an 8-kilometre (5-mile) tidal channel, The Narrows. With a total area of more than 150 square kilometres (58 square miles), the Lough is 8 kilometres (5 miles) across and 31 kilometres (19 miles) long. Its coast is so indented that the total shoreline is roughly 240 kilometres (150 miles) long – over a third of the entire coastline of Northern Ireland. A deep channel, up to 60 metres (197 feet) deep, runs almost the whole length of the central part of the loch, but most of it is less than 20 metres (66 feet) deep. Its name comes from the ancient Viking name Strangfjo'orthr, or Strong Fjord.

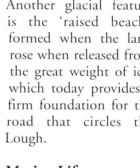

Ice Age Relics

The many small, low, rounded hills or 'drumlins' around the Lough were moulded from rock debris by glaciers during the last great Ice Age. As the ice retreated 'swarms' of drumlins were left behind,

Top left: A crab fisherman with his catch on Strangford Lough.

popularly known as 'baskets of eggs' on account of their shape. Many more were partly submerged when the area was drowned by seawater, forming low, grassy islands. Despite a local myth that there are as many of these as days in the year, there are actually just over 120. Other features include sandy beaches, rocky outcrops, and shallow reefs known as 'pladdies'.

Parts of the shore are strewn with huge 'erratics', boulders deposited when the ice sheets retreated. Another glacial feature is the 'raised beach', formed when the land rose when released from the great weight of ice, which today provides a firm foundation for the road that circles the Lough.

Marine Life

Strangford Lough is famed for its rich marine life. Over 2,000 species of marine animals – 75 per cent of all those recorded from Northern Ireland – have been found, including several unique communities of invertebrates. This includes over 300 species of molluscs, 60 per cent of all those recorded in Ireland's inshore waters.

There are at least 12 different invertebrate communities, ranging from the brightly coloured assemblages of hydroids, sponges, anemones and the soft coral Dead Man's Fingers in The Narrows, living on great quantities of food brought by the fast-flowing current, to the burrow-dwelling Norway Lobster (Scampi) in the fine mud of the deep central channel.

Beds of Horse Mussels thrive in the channels between the islands and the central channel,

Location: Runs inland from west coast of Northern Ireland, 21 km (13 miles) south east of Belfast.

Climate: Mild, with generally frost-free winters; one of the driest parts of Ireland.

When to Go: Birds and other wildlife life all year; September–October best, including huge flocks of Brent Geese.

Access: Roads around the lough; smaller roads to lakeside. North west: turn left off A22 (southbound) just after Comber and follow signs to Castle Espie WWT Centre. South west: Quoile Pondage NNR via A22 through Killyleagh, over Quoile Bridge, left and left again, following signs for Strangford; Countryside Centre well signposted.

Permits: None. Admission charge to non-WWT members at Castle Espie. Restricted access to much of Quoile Pondage NNR.

Equipment: No special equipment required.

Facilities: Hotels, B&Bs, hostels, camp/caravan sites, self-catering accommodation, especially in Newtownards, Downpatrick, Portaferry, and Bangor, 8 km (5 miles) to north; book in advance in season. Boats for hire, cruises, yacht charters and scuba diving facilities. Castle Espie visitor centre. Exhibition centre at Quoile Countryside Centre.

Watching Wildlife: Huge numbers of wildfowl/waders in autumn/winter; one of Europe's richest sites for marine life.

Visitor Activities: Birdwatching, botany, other wildlife interests, geology, sailing, diving, angling, walking, cycling.

Right: *Part of a flock of pale-bellied Brent Geese, Strangford Lough's star attraction in autumn and early winter.*

Below: *The Narrows, viewed from the attractive little fishing village of Strangford.*

which includes 'touch tanks' enabling visitors to stroke sea anemones, starfish, rays and other animals. It is Northern Ireland's only public aquarium and seal sanctuary: sick or orphaned Common Seals are rehabilitated and released into the wild.

One of Ireland's largest colonies of these seals breed on the Lough's islands, and Harbour Porpoises and Pilot Whales are often seen. Killer Whales visit occasionally, while huge but harmless Basking Sharks, the second largest fish in the world, cruise the entrance to the Lough.

Impressive Birdlife

Strangford Lough is marvellous for birdwatching, especially in winter. The immense volume of water that pours in twice daily from the Irish Sea brings with it a vast bounty of marine creatures that, together with marine vegetation, attracts thousands of birds. About 40 per cent of the Lough's area consists of huge intertidal mudflats, the most important site in Europe for wintering pale-bellied Brent Geese from Arctic Canada. Up to three-quarters of the entire world population return here from late August, peaking at 10,000–12,000 birds in October. The birds devour the extensive Eelgrass beds; some then turn their attention to the tubular green seaweed, Gutweed, while many disperse southwards to other Irish wetlands. A good place to

thought to have been there since the last Ice Age, and supporting a rich attached fauna. Burrowing sea-cucumbers and Queen Scallops find shelter between the clumps of mussels. In the north east they provide a substrate for Variegated Scallops, unknown elsewhere in the British Isles.

The Lough is popular with divers, a particularly productive site being the wreck of the Second World War Liberty ship *Empire Tana* in The Narrows. Goldsinny, Ballan and Cuckoo Wrasses can be found, while Conger Eels peer out from the wreck. Yarrell's Blennies and Spiny Squat Lobsters lurk nearby. This varied marine life can also be seen at close quarters at Exploris, an impressive aquarium,

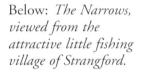

see them is Castle Espie: this Wildfowl & Wetlands Trust reserve also has the largest captive collection of wildfowl in Ireland.

The Lough has been an internationally important site for wintering Wigeon, with numbers peaking at over 20,000 in 1971–2. They arrived in these huge numbers from North and Eastern Europe, but have declined to today's peak numbers of around 2,000. Compared with Brent Geese, the Wigeon are far more affected by increased human disturbance and as a consequence cannot obtain enough food. Other ducks, however, still occur in nationally important numbers.

Up to 45,000 waders winter here, or stop over on spring and autumn migrations. These include Knot and Redshank, and large numbers of Oyster-catchers, Lapwings, Golden Plovers, Curlews, Dunlin and Bar-tailed Godwits. Summer brings a range of visitors: the huge shoals of Sand Eels provide plenty of food for the colonies of terns that breed on the islands. Gulls, too, are abundant, with Black-headed Gulls forming the largest colonies.

In the south-west corner the freshwater lagoon of Quoile Pondage (NNR) was created in 1957 by a barrage across the River Quoile. It attracts a great diversity of birds, from Greenshank and Spotted Redshank pausing on migration to breeding Sandwich, Arctic and Common Terns.

Left: *The attractive Velvet Swimming Crab, with its bright red eyes, has a shell covered with fine, velvety hair. It is capable of attacking and eating smaller crabs.*

Left: *Smaller than the Common Octopus, the Lesser or Curled Octopus rarely grows to more than 50 cm.*

SUMMARY OF CONSERVATION AREAS

The following is a selection of some of the best conservation areas in Britain and Ireland. When planning a trip, check the 'Visitor Information' panels given for each area described in the book and contact the appropriate authority (see page 172). Abbreviations are as follows:

CEC   Crown Estates Commissioners property
FC   Forestry Commission reserve
FSC   Field Studies Council centre
MNR   Marine Nature Reserve
NNR   National Nature Reserve
NP   National Park
NR   statutory Nature Reserve (Republic of Ireland)
NT   National Trust property
NTS   National Trust for Scotland property
RF   Refuge for Fauna (Republic of Ireland)
RSPB   Royal Society for the Protection of Birds nature reserve
SAM   Scheduled Ancient Monument
WT   local Wildlife Trust reserve
WWT   Wildfowl & Wetlands Trust centre

England

Arne (526 ha/1,300 acres). RSPB. Dorset. Splendid heathland and bogs, with rich flora and fauna, all six British reptile species, breeding birds (including scarce Dartford Warblers and Nightjars), wildfowl and waders.

Blakeney Point, Morston & Stiffkey Marshes (1,097 ha/2,710 acres). NT. Norfolk. Shingle spit with saltmarsh, dunes and reedbeds. Breeding terns, great range of migrant birds, special plants and insects.

Brownsea Island (220 ha/550 acres). NT/Dorset WT. Dorset. Fine conifer and mixed woodland, large brackish lagoon. Latter attracts wintering Avocets, breeding terns and other interesting birds; island also noted for dragonflies, moths, Red Squirrels and Sika Deer.

Cissbury Ring (26 ha/65 acres). NT, SAM. West Sussex. Huge Iron Age hill fort, with fine chalk grassland flora and butterflies; great views.

Cley Marshes (180 ha/445 acres). Norfolk WT. Norfolk. Famed as one of the best places in Britain to see rare birds.

Dartmoor NP (954 km²/368 sq miles). Devon. Granite plateau with wild moorland and bare outcrops (tors), steep wooded river valleys, remnant ancient woods. Bog plants and insects, upland birds.

Dungeness (898 ha/2,219 acres). RSPB. Kent. Huge shingle foreland with pools. Rare plants include Nottingham catchfly. Position makes it a magnet for migrant birds and insects; breeding birds include many gulls and terns; bird observatory as well as reserve; naturalized Marsh Frogs.

Dunwich Heath and Minsmere Beach (86.5 ha/214 acres). NT. Suffolk. Important remnant of coastal heath, with special invertebrates (including glow-worms) and birds. Beach has sandy cliffs.

East Wretham Heath (141 ha/348 acres). Norfolk WT. Norfolk. Fine grassland where dwarf wildflowers are associated with special insects; lakes attract waders and wildfowl.

Exmoor NP (693 km²/267 sq miles). Devon, Somerset. High plateau with heather grass and steep wooded river valleys; varied scenery, including superb coast. Noted for Red Deer, upland birds and lichens.

Farne Islands (33 ha/82 acres). NNR, NT. Northumberland. Great views of seabird colonies and Grey Seals.

Holkham (3,851 ha/9,516 acres). NNR. Norfolk. Dunes, sand and mud flats, saltmarshes, conifers. Wild geese, seabirds, and other birds, including rare migrants; excellent for plants and insects.

Lake District NP (2,292 km²/885 sq miles). Cumbria. Majestic scenery, with England's highest mountains overlooking the famous lakes. Great range of wildlife, including Red Squirrels, upland plants, rare fish and many birds.

Leighton Moss (161 ha/398 acres). RSPB. Lancashire. Reedbeds, shallow pools, willow scrub, limestone hills and woods. Superb plant, insect and mammal life as well great range of birds, including Bitterns.

Lindisfarne (over 3,900 ha/8,650 acres). NNR. Northumberland. Atmospheric tidal island steeped in history, with fine coastal wildlife.

Lundy Island (405 ha/1,000 acres). Landmark Trust/NT/MNR. Devon. Dramatic granite cliffs, rough grassland. Breeding seabirds, migrant birds, marine life (Britain's first MNR), Bronze and Iron Age field systems.

Malham Tarn (2,900 ha/7,200 acres). NNR, FSC, NT. North Yorkshire. Habitats around the lime-rich lake include bog and fen. Fascinating mix of upland and lowland wildlife, studied by generations of naturalists.

Minsmere (930 ha/2,300 acres). RSPB. Suffolk. One of the finest of all nature reserves, with a great range of habitats and year round wildlife interest; over 230 bird species recorded annually, 85–100 breed regularly: the highest variety for an area of this size anywhere in the UK.

Morecambe Bay (2,658 ha/6,566 acres – combined with Leighton Moss). RSPB. Lancashire. Sand flats, saltmarsh, shingle, lagoons. Immense numbers of waders and wildfowl on passage and in winter, roost on reserve, plus many other birds.

New Forest (580 km²/224 sq miles). CEC/FC/Private; proposed NP. Hampshire. One of Europe's finest ancient woodlands (with much heathland), renowned for insects, plants, birds and deer.

North York Moors NP (1,436 km2/554 sq miles). North Yorkshire, Redcar & Cleveland. Magnificent heather moors. Upland wildlife includes Red Grouse.

Ouse Washes (1,350 ha/3,336 acres). RSPB/ WT for Bedfordshire, Cambridgeshire, Northamptonshire and Peterborough. Cambridgeshire; and Welney (417 ha/1,030 acres). WWT. Norfolk. Outstanding for breeding waders and wintering wildfowl, and rich in plants, invertebrates and fish.

Peak District NP (1,438 km²/555 sq miles). Derbyshire, South Yorkshire, Lancashire, Staffordshire, Cheshire. 1951. Wild moorland surrounds limestone plateau; impressive caves, large reservoirs, clear rivers and lovely woods. Superb wildflowers and wildlife.

Scilly Isles (16 km²/6.3 sq miles). AONB. Cornwall. Idyllic islands, beautiful beaches. Breeding seabirds, outstanding for migrant birds (including rarities, especially in October), subtropical plants, prehistoric sites.

Scolt Head Island (738 ha/1,824 acres). NNR. Norfolk. Sand dunes, shingle ridge and maze of saltmarshes. Breeding terns, waders and migrants, interesting plants and insects.

Slimbridge (500 ha/1,235 acres). WWT. Gloucestershire. WWT headquarters with outstanding wintering wild swans, geese and ducks as well as world's premier captive wildfowl and flamingo collection.

Snettisham (1,315 ha/3,249 acres). RSPB. Norfolk. Superb reserve on the Wash coast, attracting huge, spectacular wader roosts.

South Downs (1,375 km²/503 sq miles). AONB; Proposed NP. Hampshire/West and East Sussex. Rolling chalk downland with many special plants and insects; splendid views and easy but exhilarating walking.

The Broads NP (303km²/117 sq miles). Norfolk/Suffolk. Complex system of shallow lakes, slow-moving rivers, reeds, marshes and damp woods. Many rare plants and insects, Bitterns, Marsh Harriers, other special birds.

Titchwell Marsh (379 ha/936 acres). RSPB. Norfolk. Reedbeds and shallow lagoons attract many breeding birds, including Marsh Harriers, as well as scarce migrants and winter-visiting wildfowl.

Walberswick (508 ha/1,270 acres). NNT. Suffolk. Saltmarsh, remnant coastal heath and huge reedbed with special birds as well as plants and reptiles.

Weeting Heath (137 ha/338 acres). Norfolk WT/NNR. Norfolk. Grass heath with rare plants, insects and birds.

Wicken Fen (324 ha/800 acres). NT. Cambridgeshire. Britain's first nature reserve, still renowned for aquatic invertebrates, plants and birds.

Yorkshire Dales NP (1,769 km²/683 sq miles). North Yorkshire, Cumbria. Unique mix of farmland. moorland, rivers and woods, including outstanding limestone scenery. Wonderful wildflowers and rich fauna.

Wales

Brecon Beacons NP (1,344 km²/519 sq miles). Powys, Carmarthenshire, Rhondda-Cynon-Taff, Merthyr Tydfil, Blaenau-Gwent, Monmouthshire. Wild uplands with beautiful red sandstone mountains, lakes, fast-flowing rivers and streams, waterfalls, caves. Great range of upland wildlife.

Craig y Ciliau (63 ha/156 acres). NNR. Powys. Limestone cliffs above heath, bog and woods; caves. Rare trees and rock plants, many birds.

Cwm Idwal (398 ha/983.5 acres). NNR. Gwynedd. Mountain cwm, corrie lake, grass moorland and spectacular cliffs. Major geological site; superb arctic-alpine flora; fish, wildfowl and upland birds.

Dale Fort (1.6 ha/4 acres). FSC. Pembrokeshire. Field centre in converted military fortress on narrow peninsula in Milford Haven waterway. Perfect place to study marine life, birds, insects, plants and other wildlife.

Llanrhidian Marsh and Whiteford Burrows (514 ha/1,271 acres). NNR, NT. Swansea. Special plants and insects on dunes, slacks and saltmarsh; excellent for winter wildfowl and waders.

Newborough Warren-Ynys Llanddwyn (633 ha/1,565 acres). NNR. Anglesey. Major dune system, sandy beaches, estuaries; large conifer plantation adjacent. Noted for plants and insects, diverse birdlife.

Ogof Ffynnon Ddu (413 ha/1,020 acres). NNR. Deep cave system, with streams, waterfalls and stalactites and stalagmites. Above ground, limestone pavement, heather moor and grassland, with varied flora and fauna.

Oxwich (289 ha/714 acres). NNR. Swansea. Complete succession of habitats from seashore via dunes, dune slacks, marshes, fen, grass, scrub, woodland and clifftop grassland ensures a great range of flora and fauna.

Pembrokeshire Coast NP (620 km²/240 sq miles). Pembrokeshire. 1952. Great range of habitats in relatively small area. Marvellous coasts and islands. Renowned for seabirds, wildflowers and marine mammals.

Pennard Cliffs and Three Cliffs Bay (100 ha/258 acres). NT. Swansea. Limestone cliffs rich in fossils, range of prehistoric remains, dunes and saltmarsh, special chalk grassland flowers and butterflies.

Rhossili (215 ha/531 acres Rhossili Downs and Beach NNR only). NNR, NT, Glamorgan WT. Swansea. Cliffs, tidal island, huge sandy bay, grassy clifftops. Many special plants and marine birds.

Snowdonia NP (2,170 km²/838 sq miles). Gwynedd, Conwy. Spectacular mountains with glaciated valleys and lakes; rivers, streams, waterfalls, woods, beautiful coast. Great variety of wildlife.

St David's Head (210 ha/520 acres). NT. Pembrokeshire. Mosaic of coastal heathland and farmland above cliffs. Breeding Choughs and many other birds, superb wildflowers and insects.

Stackpole (806 ha/1,992 acres). NNR. Pembrokeshire. Stunning coastal scenery, with limestone cliffs, sea caves, blow holes, stacks and arches. Breeding seabirds, winter wildfowl at Bosherston Lakes and scarce wildflowers among clifftop turf.

Scotland

Abernethy Forest-Loch Garten (12,500 ha/30,887 acres). RSPB. Highlands. Ancient Caledonian pine forest, with special birds and other wildlife. Loch Garten famous site for breeding Ospreys.

Balranald (658 ha/1,626 acres). RSPB. Highland (island of North Uist, Outer Hebrides). Shell-sand beaches, dunes, flower-rich machair grassland, crofted farmland, marshes. Corncrakes and waders breed amid stunning displays of wildflowers.

Ben Moire Coigach (over 6,000 ha/14,825 acres). Scottish WT. Highland. Similar habitat to Inverpolly, with breeding divers, Ptarmigan and waders.

Birsay Moors and Cottasgarth (2,340 ha/5,782 acres). RSPB. Orkney Islands. Nesting birds include Hen Harriers, Great and Arctic Skuas and Short-eared Owls; Orkney Voles are common.

Cairngorm (existing NNR: over 260 km²/100 sq miles) Proposed as national park. Highland. The British Isles' largest area of mountains, with awesome scenery and a host of special plants and animals.

Coll (1,221 ha/3,017 acres). Argyll & Bute (island of Inner Hebrides). RSPB. Similar habitat to Balranald, with similar wildlife, also large numbers of White-fronted and Barnacle Geese in winter.

Fair Isle (830 ha/2,050 acres). NTS. Shetland Islands. Large seabird colonies (17 species), famous bird observatory makes a great base for seeing migrant birds, including rarities.

Fetlar (699 ha/1,727 acres). RSPB. Shetland Islands. Varied habitats include rare serpentine heathland. Superb breeding birds, including Red-throated Divers, Whimbrels, Red-necked Phalaropes, and Arctic and Great Skuas.

Inverpolly (10,856 ha/26,825 acres). NNR. Highland. One of the wildest parts of Britain, with undulating rocky moorland, boggy hollows, patches of woodland, lakes and streams. Great geological interest and special Highland wildlife, including Golden Eagle and Wild Cat.

Loch Gruinart (1,667 ha/4,119 acres). RSPB. Argyll & Bute (island of Islay). Moorland, farmland on south and west shores of lake. Superb bird-watching, famed for wintering White-fronted and Barnacle Geese.

Loch Lomond and the Trossachs (existing NNR: 416 ha/1,027 acres) Proposed as Scotland's first national park; (existing Regional Park 440 km²/2170 sq miles. Stirling, Argyll & Bute, West Dunbartonshire. Famous lake (Britain's largest freshwater lake) with wooded shores and islands amid dramatic mountain scenery. Rich and varied wildlife.

Loch of Spiggie (115 ha/284 acres). RSPB. Shetland Islands. Large shallow lake attracts terns, skuas and other birds in summer and wildfowl in winter.

Noss (313 ha/773 acres). NNR. Shetland Islands. Huge, towering sandstone sea-cliffs and moorland, with breeding seabirds and Great Skuas.

Noup Cliffs (2.4 km/1.5 miles). RSPB. Orkney Islands. Sea cliffs holding one of the highest densities of breeding seabirds in Britain.

Rum (10,684 ha/26,400 acres). NNT. Highland (island of Skye). Remarkably diverse island with dramatic sea-cliffs and mountains. Huge breeding colony of Manx Shearwaters, reintroduced White-tailed Sea-Eagles and intensively studied herd of Red Deer; wildflowers, insects.

St Abb's Head (78 ha/192 acres). Includes St Abb's and Eyemouth Voluntary MNR. Scottish Borders. Spectacular sea cliffs, grassland, lake. Outstanding for seabirds, bird migrants, insects, wildflowers and marine biology.

St Kilda (853 ha/2,107 acres). NNR, NTS. Highland (island of Outer Hebrides). Awe-inspiring scenery, with Britain's highest sea-cliffs. One of the world's finest seabird archipelagos, with its largest gannetry.

Sumburgh Head (16 ha/40 acres). RSPB. Shetland Islands. Sea cliffs with breeding seabirds, migrant birds among shrubs, quarries and stone walls, and whales and dolphins out to sea.

Unst-Hermaness (964 ha/2,382 acres). NNR. Shetland Islands. Britain's most northerly reserve, with big seabird colonies, including huge numbers of Puffins.

Ireland

Castle Espie (20 ha/50 acres). WWT. Down. Lagoons, woodland, shore with mudflats. Wildfowl (both wild and captive), waders, other birds.

Cliffs of Moher (10 km/6.2 miles). RF. Clare. Highest sea cliffs in British Isles, with impressive seabird colonies.

Giant's Causeway/Causeway Coast (1,316 ha/3,249 acres). NNR. Antrim. Spectacular hexagonal basalt columns and sculptured pillars, beautiful bays and headlands. Outstanding flora on clifftop maritime heath and grassland, saltmarsh and other plant communities at cliff base; breeding birds include Fulmars, Peregrine Falcons and Buzzards; visiting Choughs.

Killarney NP (102 km²/39.5 sq miles). Kerry. Beautiful lakes, oak and other woodlands, mountain and moorland. Rich diversity of wildlife, including ferns, unique Kerry Slug and Red Deer.

Quoile Pondage Basin (195 ha/482 acres). NNR. Down. Freshwater lagoon, flood meadows, woodland. Breeding birds include Great Crested Grebe, Shelduck, Gadwall; great variety of waders on passage/in winter.

Rathlin Island Cliffs (4 km/2.5 miles), RSPB, and Kebble (123 ha/303 acres), NNR. Antrim. Dramatic cliffs and stacks host Northern Ireland's largest seabird colony, containing a quarter of a million seabirds; also breeding Buzzards, Peregrine Falcons and Ravens.

Strangford Lough (1,004 ha/2,482 acres). NNR/NT, MNR. Down. Includes Castle Espie and Quoile Pondage Basin. Glorious varied landscapes around this huge sea lough, with classic rounded drumlins (glacial hills). Renowned for birdlife (especially wintering pale-bellied Brent Geese, other wildfowl, and waders) and unique communities of marine invertebrates. Also seals, Harbour Porpoises and Basking Sharks.

The Burren NP (16.73 km²/6.46 sq miles). Clare. Outstanding area of karst limestone scenery, with unique mix of wildflowers in glorious profusion and interesting snail and other invertebrate fauna.

Wicklow Mountains NP (200 km²/77 sq miles). Wicklow. Includes Glendalough and Glenealo Valley NRs. Wild, rugged granite mountains with fine oak woods, conifer plantations, moorland, lakes and blanket bog. Many interesting plants, including bog and water plants, ferns, mosses and liverworts; major deer populations and good upland and woodland birds.

USEFUL ADDRESSES

Amateur Entomologists' Society
PO Box 8774, London SW7 5ZG
Tel: 07788 163 951
e-mail: aes@theaes.org
website: www.theaes.org

Bat Conservation Trust
15 Cloisters House, 8 Battersea
Park Road, London SW8 4BG
Tel: 020 7627 2629
Fax: 020 7627 2628
e-mail: enquiries@bats.org.uk
website: www.bats.org.uk

Botanical Society of the British Isles
Alex Lockton
66 North Street
Shrewsbury SY1 2JL
Tel: 01743 343789
e-mail: alex@whild.icom_web.com
website: www.bsbi.org.uk

British Dragonfly Society
Secretary, the Haywain
Hollywater Road, Bordon
Hants GU35 0AD
e-mail: thewains@ukonline.co.uk
website: www.dragonflysoc.org.uk

British Trust for Ornithology
National Centre for Ornithology
The Nunnery, Thetford
Norfolk IP24 2PU
Tel: 01842 750 050
Fax: 01842 750 030
e-mail: info@bto.org
website: www.bto.org

BTCV (formerly British Trust for
Conservation Volunteers)
36 St Mary's Street, Wallingford
Oxfordshire OX10 0EU
Tel: 01491 821 600
Fax: 01491 839 646
e-mail: Information@btcv.org.uk
website: www.btcv.org

Butterfly Conservation
Manor Yard, East Lulworth
Wareham, Dorset BH20 5QP
Tel: 01929 400 209
Fax: 01929 400 210
e-mail: BCWebmaster@butterfly-
conservation.org
website:
www.butterfly-conservation.org

Countryside Agency
John Dower House
Crescent Place, Cheltenham
Gloscester GL50 3RA
Tel: 01242 521 381
Fax: 01242 584 270

e-mail: info@countryside.gov.uk
website: www.countryside.gov.uk

Field Studies Council
Head Office, Preston Montford
Montford Bridge
Shrewsbury SY4 1HW
Tel: 01743 852 100
Fax: 01743 852 101
e-mail:
fsc.headoffice@ukonline.co.uk
website:
www.field-studies-council.org

Forestry Commission
231 Corstorphine Road
Edinburgh EH12 7AT
Tel: 0131 334 0303
Fax: 0131 316 4891
e-mail: enquiries@forestry.gsi.gov.uk
website: www.forestry.gov.uk

Herpetological Conservation Trust
655a Christchurch Road Boscombe
Bournemouth BH1 4AP
Tel: 01202 391 319
Fax: 01202 392 785
e-mail:
enquiries@herpconstrust.org.uk
website: www.hcontrst.f9.co.uk

Mammal Society
15 Cloisters House, 8 Battersea Park
Road, London SW8 4BG
Tel: 020 7498 4358
Fax: 020 7622 8722
e-mail: enquiries@mammal.org.uk
website: www.abdn.ac.uk/mammal

Marine Conservation Society
9 Gloucester Road, Ross-on-Wye
Herefordshire HR9 5BU
Tel: 01989 566 017
Fax: 01989 567 815
e-mail: info@mcsuk.org
website: www.mcsuk.org

The National Trust
36 Queen Anne's Gate
London SW1H 9AS
Tel: 020 7222 9251
Fax: 020 7222 5097
e-mail:
enquiries@thenationaltrust.org.uk
website: www.nationaltrust.org.uk

Plantlife
21 Elizabeth Street
London SW1W 9RP
Tel: 020 7808 0100
Fax: 020 7730 8377
e-mail: enquiries@plantlife.org.uk
website: www.plantlife.org.uk

Royal Society for the Protection of
Birds
The Lodge, Sandy
Bedfordshire SG19 2DL
Tel: 01767 680 551
Fax: 01767 692 365
e-mail: info@rspb.org.uk
website: www.rspb.org.uk

Wild Flower Society
82a High Street, Sawston
Cambridge CB2 4HJ
Tel: 01223 830 665
Fax: 01223 839 804
e-mail: wfs@grantais.demon.co.uk
website: www.rbge.org.uk/data/wfsoc

Wildfowl & Wetlands Trust
The New Grounds, Slimbridge
Glouscestershire GL2 7BT
Tel: 01453 891 900
Fax: 01453 890 827
e-mail: enquiries@wwt.org.uk
website: www.wwt.org.uk

The Wildlife Trusts
The Kiln, Waterside
Mather Road, Newark
Nottinghamshire NG24 1WT
Tel: 0870 036 7711
Fax: 0870 036 0101
e-mail: info@wildlife-trusts.cix.co.uk
website: www.wildlifetrusts.org

The Woodland Trust
Autumn Park, Dysart Road
Grantham
Lincolnshire NG31 6LL
Tel: 01476 581 135
Fax: 01476 590 808
e-mail:
enquiries@woodland-trust.org.uk
website: www.woodland-trust.org.uk

ENGLAND

English Nature
Northminster House
Peterborough PE1 1UA
Tel: 01733 455 101
Fax: 01733 455 103
e-mail:
enquiries@english-nature.org.uk
website: www.english-nature.org.uk

WALES

Countryside Council for Wales
Plas Penrhos, Ffordd Penrhos
Bangor
Gwynedd LL57 2LQ
Tel: 01248 385 500
Fax: 01248 355 782
e-mail: c.gwyn@ccw.gov.uk
website: www.ccw.gov.uk

SCOTLAND

National Trust for Scotland
Wemyss House, 28 Charlotte Square
Edinburgh EH2 4ET
Tel: 0131 243 9300
Fax: 0131 243 9301
e-mail: conservation@nts.org.uk
website: www.nts.org.uk

Scottish Field Studies Association
Kindrogan Field Studies Centre
Enochdhu, by Blairgowrie
Perthshire PH10 7PG
Tel: 01250 881 286
Fax: 01250 881 433
e-mail: kindrogan@btinternet.com
website: www.kindrogan.com

Scottish Natural Heritage
12 Hope Terrace
Edinburgh EH9 2AS
Tel: 0131 447 4784
Fax: 0131 446 2277
e-mail: enquiries@snh.gov.uk
website: www.snh.org.uk

Scottish Wildlife Trust
Cramond House
off Cramond Glebe Road
Edinburgh EH4 6NS
Tel: 0131 312 7765
Fax: 0131 312 8705
email: enquiries@swt.org.uk
website: www.swt.org.uk

IRELAND

Birdwatch Ireland
Ruttledge House, 8 Longford Place
Monkstown, Co Dublin
Republic of Ireland
Tel: +353 (0)1 280 4322
Fax: +353 (0)1 284 4407
e-mail: bird@indigo.ie
website: www.birdwatchireland.ie

Environment and Heritage
Service, Northern Ireland
Commonwealth House
35 Castle Street, Belfast BT1 1GU
Tel: 028 9054 6450
Fax: 028 9054 6660
e-mail: ehsinfo@doeni.gov.uk
website: www.ehsni.gov.uk

Dúchas, The Heritage Service
National Parks and Wildlife Division
7 Ely Place, Dublin 2
Republic of Ireland
Tel: +353 (0)1 647 3000
Lo Call: 1890 321 421
Fax: +353 (0)1 662 0283
e-mail: info@heritageireland.ie
website: www.heritageireland.ie

FURTHER READING

Asher, J., Warren, M. and Fox, R. (2001) *Millennium Atlas of Butterflies in Britain and Ireland.* OUP, Oxford.

Beebee, T. and Griffiths, R. (2000) *Amphibians and Reptiles.* HarperCollins, London.

Bellamy, D., Consultant (2000) *The Countryside Detective.* The Reader's Digest Association Limited, London.

Brooks, S. and Lewington, R. (revised. ed. 1999) *Field Guide to the Dragonflies and Damselflies of Great Britain and Ireland.* British Wildlife Publishing, Rotherwick.

Chinery, M. (3rd ed. 1997). *A Field Guide to the Insects of Britain and Northern Europe.* HarperCollins, London.

Crawford, P. (2000) *Living Britain: A Wildlife Celebration for the Millennium* (book and video). BBC Books, London.

Elphick, J. (2001) *The Birdwatcher's Handbook: a guide to the birds of Britain and Ireland.* BBC Worldwide, London.

Gauldie, R. (2000) *Globetrotter Travel Pack: Ireland.* New Holland London.

Gauldie, R. (2001) *Globetrotter Travel Pack: Scotland.* New Holland, London.

Hayward, P., Nelson-Smith, A. and Shields, C. (1996) *Collins Pocket Guide to the Sea Shore of Britain and Northern Europe.* HarperCollins, London.

Macdonald, D. and Barratt, P. (1993) *Field Guide to the Mammals of Britain and Europe.* HarperCollins, London.

Miller, P. and Loates, M.J. (1997) *Fish of Britain and Europe.* HarperCollins, London.

National Trust (2000) *Coast and Countryside Handbook.* National Trust, London.

Oddie, Bill (2001) *Bill Oddie's Birding Pack.* New Holland London.

Reader's Digest Nature Lover's Library (new ed. 2001) *Field Guide to the Water Life of Britain.* Reader's Digest Association London.

Roberts, M.J. (1995) *Collins Field Guide to the Spiders of Britain and Northern Europe.* HarperCollins, London.

RSPB (1998) *RSPB Nature Reserves: a visitor's guide.* RSPB, Sandy.

Simmonite. D. (2000) *Rock Climbing in England and Wales.* New Holland, London.

Somerville, C. (2001) *Images of Rural Britain.* New Holland London.

Somerville, C. (2001) *The Spirit of Rural Ireland.* New Holland London.

Sterry, P. et al (2001) *Photographic Guides to Birds, Butterflies, Mushrooms, Trees and Wildflowers* (separate guides). New Holland, London.

Streeter, D. and Garrard, I. (2nd ed. 1998) *Wild Flowers of the British Isles.* Midsummer Books, London.

Tipling, D. (revised. ed. 2000) *Top Birding Spots in Britain and Ireland.* HarperCollins, London.

ACKNOWLEDGEMENTS

AUTHOR'S ACKNOWLEDGEMENTS

First, I must thank the many naturalists, conservationists and others whose knowledge, wisdom and encouragement have informed and sustained me over the years, especially Tony Angell, Robert Burton, Mark Cocker, Tony Hare, Peter Hope-Jones, Rob Hume, Norman Jones, Hal Robinson, the Walton family, Royston Wood, John Woodward and Peter Way. I am forever grateful to my parents Walter and Mimi and my brothers Richard and Michael for instilling in me a love of nature and wild places that will never leave me.

I am also indebted to the many individuals and organizations too numerous to mention but without whose help and generosity in supplying information the book would not have been possible. Inevitably, a book such as this also depends on the work of countless others, and I have gained much from reading what they have written on a huge range of topics, from the distribution of the Snowdon lily to the origin of the Norfolk broads. Some of these reference sources are included in the list of Further Reading on page 172, but space precludes the mention of many more.

Special thanks are due to the photographer David Tipling for his beautiful and carefully chosen pictures that grace the book and add so much to its appeal: just one look at one of his dramatic landscapes or dynamic portraits of an animal or plant is enough to transport me back in time and place to memorable days in the field.

At New Holland, I am grateful to Jo Hemmings, who persuaded me to write the book, to Mike Unwin for guiding me through the initial stages, to Sue Viccars for her sensitive editing, to Alan Marshall for his skill in designing it, and especially to Camilla MacWhannell for the intelligence, patience and understanding she showed throughout its gestation.

Thanks are due to the many friends and relatives who extended the hand of hospitality during my travels researching this book, especially Becky Brown and family, Angela Boobyer and Bob Brown, Richard Elphick, Michael and Jean Elphick, John and Adrienne Howes, Frances Evans, Katy, Mark and Eva Heath, John and Tom Makin, Christine Noble, Chris and Helen Pellant and family, Veritee Reed, Geraldine O'Riordan, John, Veronica and Shelley Walton, Jude, David and J.J. Welton, Cynthia, Jack and Sue Willcock.

Finally, I owe a huge debt of gratitude to my family – my wife Melanie and children Alys, Tom and Becky – for their patience and forebearance during the long hours when I was shut away in my study writing, and for the numerous times when (often at short notice) I was away on trips to many parts of these beautiful islands; thanks also to Melanie for acting as a sounding board for the first drafts of various chapters. To them I dedicate this book.

PHOTOGRAPHER'S ACKNOWLEDGEMENTS

Throughout my travels in pursuit of photographs for this book, a multitude of National Parks' staff gave me invaluable assistance. My thanks to the following organisations and individuals: Scottish Natural Heritage; RSPB; Wildfowl & Wetlands Trust; National Trust; P&O Ferries; Caledonian MacBrayne; Hertz and Jersey European; Hugh Harrop and Shetland Wildlife; Jonathan Wills; Tom Jamieson; Anna North; Michelle Whistler; Peter Cairns; Paudie O'Leary (Killarney NP); Eric Edwards and the Broads Authority (How Hill, Norfolk); Chris Knights; Jari Peltomaki; Frederic Desmette. Special thanks to Tom & Evie Ennis for their hospitality and invaluable help in Ireland.

PHOTOGRAPHIC CREDITS

All the photographs in this book were taken by David Tipling with the exception of the following:
Swift Imagery: (Brian Radford) p23; (Gordon Hill) p33 (t); (Chris Millington) p81.
David Wilkinson: p25
Lawson Wood: p14 (br); p127 (bl, br); p142; p144 (tl, bl); p169 (tr, cr).
Windrush Photos: (Richard Revels) p14 (bc); p28 tl; p50 (t); p58; p63 (t); p65 (br); p70 (t); p96 (b); (John Roberts) p117 (tr); (Arthur Morris) p22 (bl); (Ian Fisher) p24 (b); (Gary Huggins) p26; (Roger Tidman) p27 (cl); (Colin Carver) p36; (George McCarthy) p39 (t).
www.britainonview.com: p29 (b).

INDEX